Mindful School Libraries

Mindful School Libraries

Creating and Sustaining Nurturing Spaces and Programs

Wendy Stephens

LIBRARIES
UNLIMITED®
An Imprint of ABC-CLIO, LLC
Santa Barbara, California • Denver, Colorado

Library of Congress Cataloging-in-Publication Data

Names: Stephens, Wendy, author.
Title: Mindful school libraries : creating and sustaining nurturing spaces
  and programs / Wendy Stephens.
Description: Santa Barbara, California : Libraries Unlimited, [2021] |
  Includes bibliographical references and index.
Identifiers: LCCN 2020020563 (print) | LCCN 2020020564 (ebook) | ISBN
  9781440875274 (paperback) | ISBN 9781440875281 (ebook)
Subjects: LCSH: School libraries—Administration. | Libraries and teachers.
  | School librarian participation in curriculum planning. | School
  librarians—Professional relations. | Affective education.
Classification: LCC Z675.S3 S78 2021 (print) | LCC Z675.S3 (ebook) | DDC
  025.1978—dc23
LC record available at https://lccn.loc.gov/2020020563
LC ebook record available at https://lccn.loc.gov/2020020564

ISBN: 978-1-4408-7527-4 (paperback)
      978-1-4408-7528-1 (ebook)

25 24 23 22 21   1 2 3 4 5

This book is also available as an eBook.

Libraries Unlimited
An Imprint of ABC-CLIO, LLC

ABC-CLIO, LLC
147 Castilian Drive
Santa Barbara, California 93117
www.abc-clio.com

This book is printed on acid-free paper (∞)

Manufactured in the United States of America

Contents

Introduction

DEFINING MINDFULNESS

From autonomous sensory meridian response (ASMR) voice-overs from Madison Avenue to aspirational wellness and spiritual enlightenment themes peppering the mainstream media, aspects of mindfulness seem to be everywhere at the moment. But mindfulness is much more than a feel-good marketing ploy. Mindfulness can best be understood as a portmanteau that reflects greater consciousness of one's own physical, mental, and emotional states. Its techniques can be of benefit to most people, but most especially developing minds and those with stressful and care-giving professions, like teachers and librarians. This makes incorporating aspects of mindfulness a natural fit for inherently supportive spaces like school libraries. In learning ways to hack your consciousness and share those techniques, you can begin to liberate yourself from minutiae, cultivate greater focus, and save your energies for the many things that truly matter.

At its root, mindfulness involves focusing one's attention on the present moment, while also being conscious of, and attentive to, this awareness. This sort of meta-awareness emerged from Eastern religious practice. The *Oxford English Dictionary* links usage of mindfulness to Buddhism while noting that "from the late 20th century, increasingly taught and practised outside these contexts as a formal discipline, often involving meditation with a focus on, or acknowledgement of, one's emotions, thoughts, and bodily sensations" (*Oxford English Dictionary*, "Mindfulness").

In its current incarnation, mindfulness has been closely linked to the concept of self-care as developed and promoted by intersectional political movements, including the holistic approach to health pioneered by radical political groups like the Black Panthers, as growing distrust in institutionalized medicine led to greater interest in preventative care, alternative approaches, and the mind-body connection (Boyle 2018). The roots of self-care are often linked to Audre Lorde's often-cited reflection that "caring for myself is not self-indulgence, it is self-preservation, and that is an act of political warfare" (1988, 130). Reflection is a necessity that can be represented by an allusion to the need to "secure your own oxygen mask first," evoking the boilerplate airline safety briefing. But by the time you need that mask, isn't it too late? I believe mindfulness involves being proactive and positive rather than licking the wounds imposed upon you by the world.

WHY NOW?

After the great quantification of education that marked the data-driven No Child Left Behind era of the early twenty-first century, it is not surprising that we have come back around to focus on children's affective needs. The reactionary post–Sandy Hook climate emphasizing safety, security, and student-centeredness has evolved to a point where one of the latest trends is social-emotional learning (SEL), "the process through which children and adults understand and manage emotions, set and achieve positive goals, feel and show empathy for others, establish and maintain positive relationships, and make responsible decisions" (Collaborative for Academic, Social, and Emotional Learning [CASEL] 2020). These concerns are present in the school library literature through synonyms and related concepts like brain-friendliness, the duty of care, Lynne Evarts's "library as sanctuary," and the application of concepts from the field of social work. It is true that school libraries are unique in the level and variety of personalized support they provide for teachers and students in their buildings. And unlike instructional delivery personalized based on metrics, SEL is based on ongoing interpersonal interactions across a broad population. It has been an inability to quantify those aspects of the school library program, the facets that fundamentally enrich school experiences for many children and perhaps are the sole feature making it bearable for a few, that are partially to blame for the attrition of administrative support for the school library function in many public schools. Whole-child approaches naturally appreciate the value in having the many services and supports that school libraries provide, but in siloed settings, libraries and other services can appear unlinked to educational attainment. In looking

The Ivy
BOOKSHOP

5928 Falls Road
Baltimore, MD 21 209
410.377.2966
www.theivybookshop.com
Books. Baltimore. Community.

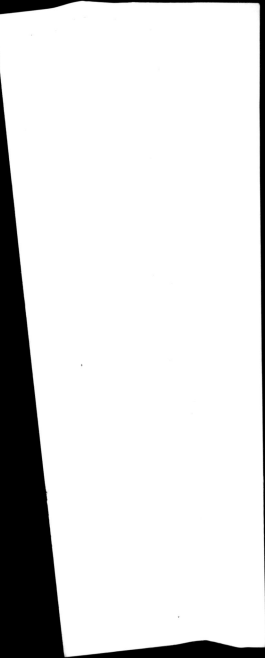

solely at outcomes, many of the variables, including school library sup-port, staffing, and programming, will not be considered as inputs. In both education and librarianship, there has emerged a near-hysterical call for increased professional advocacy through social media and policy-maker outreach. Few professions are told to devote as many resources, both time and material, to arguing for their ongoing necessity. The value of your work cannot be captured in a 280-character post or elevator speech, and it diminishes the nature of your role to attempt it.

WHY LIBRARIES?

School libraries are uniquely positioned to promote mindfulness, awareness, and community health within school communities, just as schools are positioned to construct future communities of healthy and well-adjusted citizens. Ideally, school libraries should be a laboratory of radical trust, individual support, and collective experience. In many set-tings, constraints have kept the library from embodying this role. Attend-ing to the library mindfully means identifying those barriers, articulating them, and working to identify alternatives.

In many cases, a beginning librarian or one new to the school enters the space "cold," without ongoing staffing or consultation on the role of the library in the educational enterprise in this building. And while there are policies, procedures, and other structural decisions that are the unique purview of the library professional, the school library will always reflect the instructional and cultural priorities of the school building and system administration. There are hundreds of decisions any school librarian will make in their first year. Will they renew the periodicals subscriptions without adjustment? What about standing orders and reference materials? What about circulation policies? Have they talked to their administration about research into scheduling, fixed or flexible, and how this can support the school's goals? In a mindful school setting, every policy and procedure should be weighted in consideration of whether they are really in the best interest of students, rather than the convenience of adults in the building. All regulation of the library space can be constructed to support student self-regulation. For those walking into the school library space, it is impor-tant that the space itself demonstrate that students have the agency for individual inquiry and decision making. All of that demands constant intentionality and articulation of purpose.

One stumbling block for librarians coming into schools from different settings can be the support of a service paradigm instead of an instructional paradigm. This can be especially difficult if you are moving from the classroom to the library in the same school. Librarians who have been teachers can appreciate the role of promoting independent library users and thinkers in addition to providing users with needed materials. That provision should involve, whenever possible, inculcation of information literacy, both explicitly though instruction and implicitly though interaction. While it is fine to help a student locate materials, a talk-aloud of the process can be as valuable in the long term as the information itself.

School libraries are inherently positive places and are unique in that there is little downside to their existence, between modest line items for staff, materials, and space, shared and used collectively to great effect. Because the library does deliver on relatively minor investments so successfully, there is typically little enmity to libraries outside the budget process. Any opposition the school librarian experiences is probably manufactured and easily countered. Some teachers enjoy instructing students in the research process; these should be cultivated as confederates as you support their work with resources and tools. Some parents might not support all the materials the library hold, but when they are not forced upon their children, they have little room for complaint. Even the teacher who is proudest of their own classroom library can appreciate the role of the school librarian in collecting the necessary materials for the reading practice reflected in individual student and whole-school standardized test scores.

One of my own chief concerns surrounds regular access to the library, specifically access during standardized testing. At one high school where I worked, the guidance counselor who served as test coordinator believed it easier to schedule testing in the library as we didn't have assigned classes to be displaced. At the time, our state exit exams were untimed, and students could continue testing four times each year to try to earn a diploma even after their class had graduated, factors that meant effectively closing the space for an entire week three times a year. It was a fight to have the library accessible to students during those exams, especially during the special administrations for a handful of students where the vast majority of the population was unaffected by testing. It became widely known throughout the school that I, as librarian, did not support closing the library for testing, something many classroom teachers did not understand as testing seem to them a respite. By reiterating that those who were warehoused for the duration of the exam really needed access to reading material during this noninstructional time, and since literacy was part of the school culture, I convinced the administration and testing space was eventually found elsewhere. But after that small victory, the joke was on me, because at my second school the long-time librarian had been the building test coordinator, earning extra income from orchestrating the college admissions tests, and I was forced to take on administration of AP exams in addition to achievement testing. In that setting, the library was kept open by a substitute, while I left to administer the test elsewhere— most memorably, the boys' basketball locker room. But the library remained accessible to students, so I had little latitude to complain. The important thing was that the student population had access to the materials and resources, even if services were not up to the usual standard.

In school settings where librarians have unique latitude to determine their programs and adapt their spaces, they can effectively create their own reality or accept one presented to them. I witnessed one instance of blind acceptance of status quo surrounding a librarian at a feeder school in my district. Any afternoon I had to leave school early, I saw this elementary school librarian standing out in the middle of a busy road, directing traffic for pick-up. I would thank my lucky stars that I didn't have that particular duty, assuming this was something that had been inflicted upon her by an unfeeling administration, which went on my list of one "not supportive of librarians." Then, as a district, we were preparing for accreditation, we agreed that it was important that the library should be open before and after school and wrote this into our policies and procedures. When presented with that goal, this particular librarian's principal immediately assigned that duty to someone else, and the librarian was able to man the circulation desk before and after school. The administrator did not have a particular desire to see that librarian in that role; it had simply not occurred to her that the librarian had work to do outside the school day. Not only do we need to educate our administrators about that we do, but also we need to educate them about the work that we want to do. Mindfulness practice can help us hone our priorities.

Students, like faculties, respond to how you present yourself and your work. Too many librarians position themselves in an inferior position to classroom teachers. They say apologetically they "don't have a class" or "don't have to" do whatever the classroom teacher is responsible for. Instead, they could consider themselves alongside administrators or guidance counselors, the other faculty members with graduate training, with specialized roles and whole-school responsibilities. It is up to librarians to showcase the importance and gravity of our profession and position ourselves in a long tradition of educational attainment and student-centered learning.

WHY ME?

I was weighing whether or not I would able to complete this project when, within the course of a week, three different people told me, in very different contexts, that I was "calm." I don't know if *calm* is the right term; for me, that implies a lack of passion, which I definitely possess but tend to deploy very, very selectively. But nonetheless, the trio of affirmations that I at least appeared to have mastered the appearance of being unruffled urged me on in trying to express the necessity of affective aspects of school library work. And I can't deny that *I do* feel calm. I feel similarly as I did that, according to a formula, I had only a fraction of a percent of a chance of having a cardiac event, maybe the least likelihood my doctor had ever seen. Of course, I thought, I am not going to have a heart attack because I am not in a constant reactive, flight mode. And if I am calm, it is because I always try to see the big picture. It's a function of age and experience, but also practice.

If I do seem calm, it is because the vast majority of the time, I can slow down and avoid knee-jerk reactions. I have worked hard on harnessing all sorts of digital and analog tools to juggle the many aspects of librarianship, and also adopting mental hacks to create a level of ambient awareness that keeps me from too-blatant manipulation of my reptilian brain. I have made some radical decisions when it comes to how to allot my attentions and have systematized many of the routine tasks in my life to the point where they no longer intrude upon my awareness. This took a couple of decades of real work—wide reading, trial and error around productivity strategies, self-care, and the radical candor enabled by time and perspective—to get me to a place where I might have something to share around this topic.

As I enter my fifth year in higher education, the thing most palpable for me when I return to K–12 campuses now is an overwhelming and free-floating anxiety on the part of faculty, students, and even administrators. That is perfectly explicable. Everything from the partisan political atmosphere to climate collapse contributes to a generalized sensation of panic and grief. High stakes testing and constant assessment have led to stress in even the youngest students. Mindfulness strategies can allow students to manage stress, tune out distractions, and better confront authentic assessments; these work in lock-step with libraries providing practice in public speaking and other authentic presentation of work, promoting interpersonal interactions through collaborative learning spaces, and support for the range of everyday information needs students manifest.

While everyone is different and will necessarily have their own paths to self-regulation and mindfulness, I hope that in sharing a repertoire of strategies and experiences, school librarians can bring a new degree of calm to their spaces and services.

REFERENCES

Boyle, Sarah. 2018. "Remembering the Origins of the Self-Care Movement." *Bust*, June 23, 2018. https://bust.com/feminism/194895 -history-of-self-care-movement.html.

Collaborative for Academic, Social, and Emotional Learning (CASEL). 2020. "What Is SEL?" https://casel.org/what-is-sel/.

Lorde, Audre. 1988. *A Burst of Light*. Ithaca, NY: Firebrand Books.

"Mindfulness, n." OED Online. March 2020. Oxford University Press. https://www.oed.com/view/Entry/118742?redirectedFrom=mindful ness, accessed June 1, 2020.

ONE

The Library and Stress

ADVERSE CHILDHOOD EXPERIENCES AND TRAUMA

When J. D. Vance's 2016 book *Hillbilly Elegy: A Memoir of a Family and Culture in Crisis* hit the top of the *New York Times* best-seller list, I was intrigued by one aspect of the book in particular. Most readers seem to focus on Vance's harrowing childhood experiences growing up in Ohio, but the concept of adverse childhood experiences (ACE) was a new one to me then, although it seems to have gained considerable traction in the educational community since. In his memoir, Vance offers an excellent conceptual introduction to the research into ACEs, exploring how that affects young people as their brains develop.

The concept of ACEs comes from public health research. Felitti et al. (1998) developed a questionnaire about childhood experience to inform their study about whether ACEs were linked to health risk behaviors and adult diseases. ACEs proved to be prevalent in the population. The level of positive responses for their questions ranged from a low of 3 percent for a respondent's mother having been threatened with or hurt by a weapon, to the most respondents, 23.5 percent, having lived with a problem drinker or alcoholic. More than half of respondents (52%) experienced at least one category of adverse childhood exposure; 6.2 percent reported more than four exposures. With regard to the connection to health, the results were emphatic. The Felitti study found manifestations of ACEs predicted behaviors such as smoking, alcohol or drug abuse, overeating, or sexual behaviors, behaviors they theorized evolved "as coping devices in the face of the stress of abuse, domestic violence, or other forms of family and household dysfunction" (1998, 253). High levels of exposure to ACEs can be expected to produce anxiety, anger, and depression in children.

The most eye-opening thing to me as a reader was the range of abuse and neglect that were described as linked to physical and psychological damage. The range of factors documented by Felliti et al. went much beyond anything that I had ever anticipated as having these sorts of long-term implications. While a marked trauma like growing up in a war zone or living through a natural disaster might be something that would definitely have lasting psychological implications, detrimental effects on young developing children were attributable to much more common occurrences like parents divorcing or being raised in a household without emotional support.

ACEs have been proven to be cumulative, and neuroimaging has demonstrated that in the most extreme cases where children were remarkably deprived, they dramatically impede proper brain development. Add in cortisol and other stress hormones repeatedly flooding the brain, and the result is "a negative effect on a range of executive functions, weakening children's concentration, language processing, sequencing of information, decision making and memories" (Terrasi and de Galarce 2017, 37). It is not surprising that many behavioral issues have their roots in biological ones.

Given that the most young people have had one of these ACEs by the time they enter adolescence, it is absolutely necessary that educators appreciate how prevalent these adverse experiences are among young people and how this can manifest in problems with attachment, physical health, and emotional regulation. When a student is externalizing their feelings or otherwise unable to stay calm and in control, they lack the ability to focus on schoolwork. Many classroom management issues can be viewed as a manifestation of an overall lack of executive function attributable to ACEs and trauma.

THE STUDENT MENTAL HEALTH CRISIS

Many of the images of school in the common consciousness present the classroom environment as having little to nothing to do with student emotional states. Students are presumed to come fed, rested, and focused, with pencils, paper, and books, ready to learn. And schools are depicted with rows of often no more than a dozen smiling faces, smaller classrooms than any I have ever seen. None of this can be presumed in public school classrooms, and when students have experienced trauma and are in distress over fundamental lack of support, their attention can be distracted and their physiology suspended in a fight, flight, or freeze response that makes any instruction, no matter how engaging and student centered, basically ineffective. Coupling this with the realities of modern public education means that crowded classrooms give teachers less time to get to know each student and providing less physical space for each student, all of which makes the relational aspect of teaching fraught.

If we look at the timeline of today's students' lives, we will see nothing but constant war, increasingly militarized security in schools and other public settings, and mounting political polarization. Team this with the fact that many middle-class families are having fewer children and feeling compelled to give each child a thorough range of opportunities and supports necessary to be viable in today's competitive workplace and tomorrow's uncertain one, and the pressure on young people becomes unprecedented. An estimated one in five students has a diagnosed mental health issue, and it is probable that many more have problems yet to be identified. The fast pace of an always-on, technology-enabled life takes a toll on children, too. In discussing the rush through childhood, Emily Kaplan (2019) writes that "young children sleep less and have far more transitions in their days than in previous generations—and I think most educators and parents would agree that their developing brains aren't really designed to cope with adult schedules and pacing."

Remembering the concept of the hierarchy of needs developed by Abraham Maslow (1943), it becomes immediately apparent how student physiological needs and safety are fundamental elements underpinning all school and other success. Maslow's hierarchy is depicted as a pyramid, emphasizing the dependence on foundational wellness. Maslow believed that physiological needs take precedence over all other needs, writing, "What this means specifically is, that in the human being who is missing everything in life in an extreme fashion, it is most likely that the major motivation would be the physiological needs rather than any others. A person who is lacking food, safety, love, and esteem would most probably hunger for food more strongly than for anything else" (Maslow 1943, 373).

A typical reaction to a trauma—a psychic wound—is hyperarousal. "Over time, such chronic stress produces neurobiological changes in the brain, which researchers have linked to poor physical health and to poor cognitive performance" (Terrasi and de Galarce 2017, 36)

Mindfulness practice is predicated on noticing what's happening in the present moment and responding with a nonreactive mind. Students who have experienced trauma become "wired for hypervigilance" and develop a "faulty alarm system" easily triggered by minor events. "For instance, someone who's been through trauma may read an expression of mild irritation as anger or interpret constructive criticism as a threat. Moreover, once their fear response is activated, it can take longer and be more difficult to calm down" (Donahoe 2018). A public school setting with between 30 and 40 students in a classroom is "already not trauma-informed. It's a very difficult context in which to build relationships, and the architecture, policies and procedures that can make schools feel institutional only make it harder" (Schwartz 2019). Adopting mindfulness may be difficult for students who have experienced trauma, according to Sam Himelstein, a clinical psychologist, who says that because even the practice of closing their eyes could trigger some students, he prefers to stress physical awareness (Donahoe 2018).

Given the realities of existing today in a world characterized by climate collapse, economic uncertainty, and aspirational social media ubiquity, childhood today is necessarily stressful. Libraries are one place where we can quiet the media stream and give students permission to be idle, to think, and to dream. Quiet time and ample space in libraries can be a luxury for overclocked student minds. This is valuable because "research also shows that children are resilient, and their brains are flexible . . . when teachers fully understand their students' needs, they can provide the physical and emotional space that support what researchers call neuroplasticity— or the brain's ability to require itself, forming new neural connections" (Terrasi and de Galarce 2017, 37). Whether it is student attitudes, academic attainment or overall classroom behavior, adopting an affective learning paradigm supports the soft-skill outcomes that are necessary components for success in academics and later the workplace.

LIBRARY ANXIETY

If you search for images of libraries online, you are introduced to the concept of the library as perceived by the public at large. Those libraries will be so large as to appear cavernous, ringed with bookshelves and almost entirely devoid of people. These open spaces can create an unsettling sense of being out of sorts. Given this cultural understanding of libraries, it is not surprising that students may experience uncertainty on where to begin to interact with this space and locate the materials that they need or want. Ideally, we can develop systems for our library to make the space more welcoming and intuitive, emphasizing natural traffic patterns and signage to create intuitive systems of finding and checking out resources. It is up to school libraries, as the first libraries so many children have experienced, to present the library as warm and inclusive and avoid providing any sensation of these spaces being relatively uninhabited, unassailable walls of books.

One way a lack of certitude can manifest is through library anxiety, a recognized phenomenon described as a fear of both the library space, which can be seen as overwhelming and confusing, and of the process of using the library to find materials. In 1986, Constance Mellon published findings from a two-year qualitative research study where 75–85 percent of college student library users described their initial response to library research in terms of fear. Students might worry that they are alone in not knowing how to use the library or may feel paralyzed when trying to start library research. Younger students can also experience stress or dread when they are given research assignments, or even uncertainty about relatively low stakes tasks like how to locate and check out materials. This experience is so ubiquitous that even the best-trained librarians can be counted among the anxious when given an information-seeking task outside their purview. Student researchers may fear approaching library staff for help or might be uncertain about whom to approach in these situations—team teaching with classroom teachers can complicate rather than clarify the process of information retrieval and technology integration.

Despite their comfort with some aspects of technology, students may experience anxiety or confusion when they try to search the catalog or negotiate databases using controlled vocabulary and indices. With as many as three of four students afflicted by some degree of anxiety related to library research, it is important for librarians to reinforce their accessibility and that they are there to be helpful. Even casual interaction can be seen as contributing to comfort in lower stakes interactions because when librarians are helpful for smaller tasks—anything from loaning the stapler to helping negotiate the networked printer—then they will become more trusted for recommendations in terms of resources or research approaches.

Why isn't a library more like a spa? This is a question I have been considering, because it seems as if when you think about the types of effects that people claim to experience after spa visits—relaxation, rejuvenation, refreshment—these are the sorts of things that are equally applicable after time spent amongst illuminating literature and a rich range of resources that individuals do not have access to at home. And as in a spa environment, participation requires trust on the part of any visitor that the practitioner will facilitate your access to appropriate materials with minimal intervention. By positioning libraries more like these types of positive experiences, institutions can allay library anxiety and also create positive associations for students that will reap benefits in terms of long-term relationships that will make it more likely for them to consult the librarian regarding academic information needs in the future.

GRIT AND RESILIENCE

It is possible to ground classroom management in trauma-informed principles "learning how to redirect, learning how to confront people with a non-aggressive pose, not taking it personally, all of that overlaps to help form a relationship," said Himelstein (Schwartz 2019). Too often *mindfulness* is presented as synonymous with *grit*, the term for persistence after failure that Angela Duckworth popularized. As a classroom teacher, Duckworth "grew less and less convinced that talent was destiny and more and more intrigued by the returns generated by effort" (Duckworth 2016). Duckworth's grit is a sort of psychological ability to rebound given adversity, and part of her analysis is identifying this as a character trait that was associated with successful individuals. When grit is presented as a characteristic to be inculcated or learned, this puts children who have already suffered adverse experiences or trauma under an undue burden to overcome learned dispositions. When, as Duckworth asserts, "what we accomplish may depend more on our passion and perseverance than on our innate talent," those who persevere are lauded as exceptional (Duckworth 2016). Resilience and ability to rebound from negative circumstances will vary greatly by individual.

Much of what we know about child development is predicated on healthy environments and relationships. Children develop more robust social-emotional capabilities when they have a chance to learn through play and through deep connections. Quality education is highly interpersonal. Caring teachers who understand child development and who know and are attuned to children in their care are far more important than many measures of quality like class size, physical environments, or a specific curriculum. Complex, open-ended conversation is critical to language acquisition and development. Children need time to experience warm, empathic, oral language in a nurturing, language-rich, and unhurried environment. This includes conversing with peers playfully, telling rambling stories to an adult, listening to a range of literature and asking meaningful questions based on stimuli and imagination. Much learning can come naturally from interpersonal conversations between parent and child. Educators, like parents, can encourage healthy connections and language acquisition open-ended questions like "Tell me about your story," rather than monitoring and assessment questions like "What are you writing?" It is obviously a labor-intensive effort and one that it is impossible to replicate via technological means.

EMOTIONAL INTELLIGENCE AND SOCIAL-EMOTIONAL LEARNING

In 1995, Daniel Goleman was the first to contextualize emotional intelligence as important as IQ for long-term success in his best seller on the topic. Stressing the critical need for self-restraint and compassion, Goleman wrote, "There is growing evidence that fundamental ethical stances in life stem from underlying emotional capacities . . . those who are at the mercy of impulse—who lack self-control—suffer a moral deficiency. The ability to control impulse is the base of will and character" (1995, xii).

The educational manifestations of what we now call social-emotional learning date back to the mid-1990s, when the first programs addressing student emotional needs gained traction, usually in response to specific concerns, like destigmatizing teen motherhood or reducing the rate of students dropping out of school, without addressing more holistic concerns. Often because of instructional siloes and other times because of funding streams and accountability measures, social-emotional learning can be fragmented and related to a single topic. At one school where I taught, a grant-funded elective course with a curriculum purported to focus on human relationships. In reality, the curriculum was a faith-based abstinence course, one very few students were interested in taking on their own. But because a dedicated family and consumer science teacher conducted three sections of this course every day, it quickly became a requirement for the only students that the guidance counselors could rationalize that it would benefit, and those were girls expecting babies. To me, this seemed a form of shaming, and it is worth noting that boys expecting babies were not scheduled into these classes. It was like shutting the stable door after the horse has bolted, and I would much rather those students had had that time to work on child development or parenting skills. Instead, students experienced an emphatically negative message about their present condition.

Self-regulation while under stress is only a very small facet of overall mindfulness. Mindfulness doesn't make judgments about whether or not something is desirable, being much more concerned with just identifying the sensation or emotion happening and choosing to manage that within the realm of acceptable behavioral outcomes. Many social-emotional learning efforts focus on naming feelings. It is more efficacious to avoid physiological reaction rather than manage it. We are teaching in a moment of increased awareness of the fundamental importance of social-emotional learning.

AN ONGOING NEED FOR EMPATHY

After the 2016 presidential election, one of our professional publications featured an image of graffiti that had been sent to the Southern Poverty Law Center to document political hostilities in school. "Build that wall" had been written on a library study room window. It was captioned as from my county, and when I looked at the room where that the image had been captured, I recognized the setting immediately. It was the northmost study room in the library where I had worked for a decade. It was particularly upsetting to know that the sort of thing was happening in a school climate that I had previously considered to be unusually safe, supportive, and inclusive. It struck me then that schools can never stop doing the work of building empathy and community, that it will be an ongoing process as long as there are new students and new teachers and new concerns cropping up.

Many of the trauma-informed practices being introduced in schools today are helpful for teachers as well as students. The next chapters will present how librarians and teachers are exploring ways to practice mindfulness, self-awareness, and emotional regulation skills in their schools on a daily basis. When teachers present their own involvement in mindfulness, unlike many social-emotional learning efforts, the effect can be one of creating a community of learners, as adults demonstrate their ongoing work to practice of emotional regulation, effective communication, and other skills they may not have learned as children, they are modeling what it looks like to heal and thrive throughout the life span.

REFERENCES

Donahoe, Emily. 2018. "Teaching with Trauma." *Edutopia*. November 20, 2018. https://www.edutopia.org/article/teaching-trauma.

Duckworth, Angela. 2016. *Grit: The Power of Passion and Perseverance.* New York: Simon and Schuster.

Felitti, Vincent J., Robert F. Anda, Dale Nordenberg, David F. Williamson, Alison M. Spitz, Valerie Edwards, Mary P. Koss, and James S. Marks. 1998. "Relationship of Childhood Abuse and Household Dysfunction to Many of the Leading Causes of Death in Adults: The Adverse Childhood Experiences (ACE) Study." *American Journal of Preventive Medicine* 14, no 4: 245–258.

Goleman, Daniel. 1995. *Emotional Intelligence: Why It Can Matter More Than IQ.* New York: Bloomsbury.

Kaplan, Emily. 2019. "What's Lost When We Rush Kids through Childhood." *Edutopia.* August 23, 2019. https://www.edutopia.org/article/whats-lost-when-we-rush-kids-through-childhood.

Maslow, A. H. 1943. "A Theory of Human Motivation." *Psychological Review* 50, no 4: 370–396. https://doi.org/10.1037/h0054346.

Mellon, Constance. 1986. "Library Anxiety: A Grounded Theory and Its Development." *College & Research Libraries* 47, no. 2 (March): 160–165. https://crl.acrl.org/index.php/crl/article/view/14195/15641.

Schwartz, Katrina. 2019. "Why Mindfulness and Trauma-Informed Teaching Don't Always Go Together." *KQED Mindshift.* January 27, 2019. https://www.kqed.org/mindshift/52881/why-mindfulness-and-trauma-informed-teaching-dont-always-go-together.

Terrasi, Salvatore and Patricia Crain de Galarce. 2017. "Trauma and Learning in America's Classrooms." *Phi Delta Kappan* 98, no. 6 (March): 35–41.

Vance, J. D. 2016. *Hillbilly Elegy.* New York: HarperCollins Publishers.

TWO

Sensory Experiences and Self-Soothing in the Library

Benefits of variable light, climate control, furnishings, quiet and collaborative spaces

THE WHIRLWIND OF SCHOOL

As the largest classroom in most school buildings, the library is a natural space for mindfulness and an antidote to one real common detriment to student wellness, the whirlwind of constant motion in the average public school building. The Pavlovian connection of stimulus and response is well understood, and the use of auditory cues in the school setting too often signals release, which is not ideal for creating a situation where the classroom and educational experience should be presented as intrinsically positive and enjoyable. The ricocheting sounds of bells can be particular pain points for those with sensory input issues.

I began my school library career on a block schedule, with four classes each day, an incredible boon to a new teacher. Students had ample time within those blocks to really delve into inquiry and digital projects. Teachers would meet their students in the library to set the stage for the class, signaling that this time period was more collaborative and social in nature. Early in my tenure at that school, the administration made the sage decision to eliminate the bells signaling the beginning and ending of each of the four lunch periods. They were correct that classes knew inherently when to go and come, and there was little distraction. This system worked so well that when some of the block classes were split to accommodate a yearlong Advanced Placement schedule, that passing time in the middle of the block was not marked with bells, either. Nonetheless, students instinctively began moving toward the door at the appointed hour and almost always got to class on time.

When I began working at another school with seven periods a day, I felt myself unable to sink into the experience of concentrated flow, neither when helping students researching or working on projects nor with my own work, not with those bells signaling the change every 50 minutes. If teachers met their classes in the library instead of walking them in from the classroom, it was largely because it was the only way they could hope to get anything accomplished in such a short research session. Not only were the sounds of the bells physically jarring, but the sense of hustle that the frequent changes involved seemed to be equally psychologically detrimental. I never adjusted to an accelerated schedule, and I could see that difference manifested in student behavior. And for students deemed to be "at risk," they may experience even more transitions during the day as they leave the class for supportive services. It is not surprising that when elementary students begin leaving a dedicated classroom for specific content-area instruction, anecdotal reports suggest that behavioral issues can spike.

WHAT MAKES FOR A MINDFUL LIBRARY SPACE?

Is your space mindful? In the school setting, I would argue that this is one of those things you, your teachers, and students instinctively know upon entering a place. Has everything been carefully considered that is a part of this environment? Has shared ownership been established and expressed? From the types of information posted around the space, to the way that books and other materials are made accessible to visitors, the library's fundamental values are effectively on display.

It can be helpful to think of the distinction between the classroom and library as the distinction between a second place with a predictable role and that of a third place with less structure and fewer strictures. The "third place" is a term sociologist Ray Oldenburg (2000) used to refer to places where people spend time between home and work. Third places are typically locations where individuals can come together to exchange ideas, interact, and build relationships. For connected young people, online applications from Instagram to WhatsApp groups to collaborative Google docs can be seen as third places. But as Oldenburg notes, the most effective places for building real community seem to be physical places where people can easily and routinely interact. The sense of welcome and logical flow within a school media center can promote intentional communities that are both impromptu and sustained. If the library space makes sense, and is immediately explicable, this can help reduce that sensation of unease that underpins library anxiety and creates a "third place" rather than a liminal one.

As professionals, we often inherit spaces designed by other people, sometimes ones designed for other uses entirely. In the first school where I worked as a librarian, the library space was almost new when I accepted the position. It was very much a product of the turn of the millennium, dominated by a dozen heavy computer pressboard stations necessitated by heavy central processing units (CPUs) and cathode-ray tube (CRT) monitors.

Everyone at the school was quite proud of the space because the library had previously been in a dark interior room that was now the football team's weight training facility, while the newer library space was the conspicuous centerpiece of the new second floor of the school building. The library extended over a porte cochere, looking out across farmland across the street, and was a visible presence for the school as community members drove back and forth along the main artery adjacent to the campus. As I worked there over a decade, some of the shortcomings of the impressive but economical design and construction made themselves evident. That space was created at the moment the ubiquity of computing, and the number of electrical outlets and network connections was very limited, resulting in unsafe daisy chains of surge protectors and extension cords that had demanded constant adjustment. Another issue was the number of skylights and windows facing west; it was almost impossible to achieve dimness, to say nothing of darkness, in the space, and that was compounded by the fact that all of the lights were on a single circuit, turned on with fork like key too often accompanied by a dramatic statement about "letting there be light." What had seemed a convenience at the point of construction—all of the lights on a single switch—became difficult when using a digital projector became commonplace, even though I strategically located it in the dimmest corner of the space.

Natural light is important for well-being and should be preserved at all cost. When I was in school myself, the energy crisis of the late 1970s manifested in boarding or bricking over windows of public buildings to save on climate control. It was interesting to see that most of the schools with discretionary spending removed this makeshift insulation in the 1990s, leaving other, less prosperous campuses literally walled off. Do lumens equal attention? This was the assertion at a professional development workshop I attended, which suggested that strategies for active viewing of video involve both leaving the lights on and stopping the film periodically to ask probing questions and to reassert focus. Watching with the lights on signals that notes should be taken, just as if it were another type of instructional activity and not the darkness at noon that leads to sleepy, almost anesthetized students when the class changed. I used this to help rationalize the fact that the digital projector was very hard to see given the light, natural and artificial, in the space.

Eventually, our plant manager was able to isolate the lights into two separate switches, which gave us a lot more flexibility in terms of lighting and thus the types of events that we could comfortably host in the library. Our coffee house poetry slams definitely benefited from a little bit more ambience, and technology demonstrations were much easier to deliver and perceive.

Another issue beginning to show itself was the bowing of the economical pressboard bookshelves. Our enrollment had grown, as had our collection, and the shelves which were once relatively bare began to groan under the weight of new additions to the collection. The laminate shelves were not up to the weight of that shift, and we had begun flipping them upside down periodically to counteract that effect.

I had been working in this sort of predigital space for about a decade, when a colleague got in touch because her high school was looking to build a new showpiece library. She wanted my input, and I sent her my pie-in-the-sky ideas for an up-to-date facility. A few months later, she got in touch to let me know that she was planning on retiring. She wanted to know if I wanted to continue to work on that building project as the librarian. This school was in a district that had local funding based on both property and local sales tax, which is unusual in our area; I would also have the opportunity to work with a superintendent I knew well and respected. My long-time principal has just retired, and knowing that I would never have the opportunity to create an independent vision of what a school library space could be in my current cash-strapped district, I embraced that opportunity and took a leap of faith in moving to the other high school.

I spent the first year at my new school working in the older facility, which had been very modern when constructed 60 years earlier. It was a stand-alone library building with two outside doors at either end. The retiring librarian had been there for more than 40 years, and I immediately perceived there was a lot to be done to update this space for contemporary students. After a year in this building, the shelving and collection were moved to what was an industrial arts woodworking shop in a metal building on our campus. Keeping the library accessible to students meant I had to remove all of the books and maintain them in order while the old shelving was removed and transported to their new location, then shift the collection.

The library would remain in the woodshop for a little bit more than a year. Individual students found their way there, but teachers did not like the claustrophobic sensation, and as the walls did not reach the ceiling, it was difficult to provide instruction that did not ricochet through the rest of building. The faculty was surprised I had made the effort to set up a library at all, and with facilities issues like a leaking roof and inadequate climate control, every day presented a new challenge. I was determined to keep the collection accessible, but I often had to leave the library for instruction and the library was constrained to the point where it was no longer really a browsable collection.

If you are working from a temporary space, I urge you to strongly consider which aspects of the collection are most critical to the functioning of the library, and mindful spaces should always have the high interest materials—new books, graphica, magazines—close at hand. The newly constructed library was a two-story structure with a central fireplace and a wraparound second floor. In the new space, fiction was downstairs, while the lesser-used nonfiction was relegated to the upstairs shelving. Though I expressed a real desire to interfile reference, which circulated, with nonfiction, the architect and interior designer did not take this into account.

Many who have seen that library say it reminds them of the space in the classic John Hughes movie *The Breakfast Club,* set in the New Trier High School library. The first floor was also ringed with glassed-in study rooms and the computer lab. The school sits at a prominent intersection, and the glass windows ensured community observation of the facility from the street. Complementary facilities include a fenced exterior courtyard, a coffee shop, and an adjacent lecture hall with a 300-person capacity. In the small community where my high school was located, the construction project was a major news topic; it made the first page of the daily paper several times. The actual execution left much to be desired—the study rooms did not feature any ventilation, and got teenage-funky almost immediately, and a vent was aimed directly at my seat at the circulation desk, something that ended up giving me an ulcer on my pupil. And there were parabolically curved shelves, something I can never recommend.

I did assert that I wanted lots of collaborative workspaces, and I wanted a circulation desk that didn't belong to the staff or to the guests in the same way that when you walk into an Apple store The Genius Bar doesn't seem to belong to anyone in particular. Instead of dedicating computer workstations for the library catalog, we decided to mount tablets with catalog access around the library. Each of the study rooms was designed with a hot-swappable monitor, so students could share their digital work from their school-issued iPads. This relatively simple investment in display made the spaces much more inviting for group work. The integrated computer lab had iMacs which could be used for more intensive computing needs.

Two library moves within the space of a year-and-a-half was one of the most challenging things that I've ever done, but it did give me the opportunity to practice something I have always believed is valuable in libraries and in life: working with a relatively blank canvas. I believe every librarian could benefit from removing every single item from their library and considering it in turn. Is it necessary for your library practice? Is it something that has been improved upon in the 40 years since it was created? Is it something that can be supplanted by another device?

Even if you don't have the opportunity to design your own space, feel empowered to make changes to the physical plant. One of the things I have noticed often happens to librarians is "inheriting" a lot of things. Libraries are chockablock with orphaned items left behind that occupy corners and shelves, or forgotten signage. Too often these things are no longer needed, and maybe no one even remembers how they came to be there. I visited a high school library where there was a strange desk in the corner of the library. I asked how it was used, and the librarian said that someone had used the spot to work one-on-one with a special education student. That student had graduated, but that desk was still there in the corner, as if anticipating that they might return. In the meantime it added visual clutter and really struck an incoherent note.

VISUAL INFORMATION INVENTORY

The best use of decor in the school library can be as a teachable moment. When visiting students are in a highly suggestible state, in a third space that is not the classroom or the home, they are ripe for instruction through visual information. Don't think you must have a generous budget to develop intellectually stimulating library spaces. At many conferences, you can find free posters of the U.S. presidents, award-winning books, and other reference sources in visual format. Many local organizations can likely provide local maps; state parks are an excellent resource in this regard, as are local Chambers of Commerce and tourist information clearinghouses. One of the more effective and interesting library decorations I've encountered showcased the text of historic markers from the community. One resource I particularly recommend are the posters that promote a series of books by listing alphabetically ordered words for the college bound. I often saw students "testing themselves" by reviewing those posters. Even when they are not aware of the meaning, repeated exposure to those undefined terms will make the new vocabulary, when encountered in text, "sticky."

Consider every aspect of your library that students will encounter, which might involve experiencing lower sightlines. Even your technology can provide a passive exposure to information. Our state's online collection of digitized primary source images were our screensavers. We loaded local history information on tablets for in-library consultation at stationary kiosks, offering some short but compelling reading for those at a loose end, who might not be sure what they want, or even if they want, to read.

Do not underestimate the effect of having high-interest information posted and available. My first paraprofessional aide was an enthusiastic sports fan, and the first week on the job, I noticed that despite describing herself as not being a reader, she avidly followed the school teams' appearances in the local newspapers. I asked her to cut out every mention of our school, laminate those pieces of newsprint, and post them in the library. I can say emphatically that many students stopped by at the library daily just to see the new headlines. At some points, we printed news off the Internet to include that as well.

This feature proved so popular that, during one particularly winning football season, we also duplicated the news coverage for dissemination via the library circulation desk. Many reluctant, below grade-level readers were among those stopping by every Monday to read the coverage of the last game. Eventually, my paraprofessional aide began making additional copies of the news articles to post in other spaces as the administration noticed how successful this happened to be at attracting students.

In one of the schools where I taught, every classroom was expected to have a word wall of content area vocabulary. To support adolescent literacy in general and promote the library more specifically, I developed my own word wall with more than 80 words, printed these on yellow paper and cut them into slips that I laminated and attached with double-sided tape to the circulation desk—everything from *controlled vocabulary* to *virtual private network*. For the faculty entering the library, this helped reinforce that I was a specialist with command of a particular set of skills. And, as in subject area classrooms, by frequent exposure to these terms, students were bound to recognize them when I used them in instruction or conversation and were more likely to retain them.

There are many free online graphic design tools and interesting fonts available that can be leveraged to make information more visually appealing. But be deliberate in your informational décor and do not fall victim to the trap of displaying scolding signs posted around the library. Some schools require posting of a lot of boilerplate information in every classroom, and these are usually the spaces with blanket policies and procedures throughout the school building. Other educational philosophies stress the independent creation and posting of rules particular to an instructional space and community. Whatever your library "rules," they should mirror those of the larger school, with very few additions possible depending on local staffing and solid supervision provisions. Policies or any other print materials you display for students should be worthy of framing or heavy-duty lamination at the very least. There are few things more dispiriting than a crumbling, duplicated sign on a piece of paper hanging from Scotch tape.

BEYOND DÉCOR

We all have an aspirational library ideal, a Pinterest board of what we want to incorporate. For years, I dreamed about a whiteboard tree with digital picture frames representing equidistant "blooms" after seeing the one at Chicago Public Library's YouMedia lab for teens. I could never convince our plant manager to cut up what he considered a perfectly good whiteboard with his jigsaw for this purpose.

I have visited libraries where there were absolutely no decorations, where you could have been in an urgent care clinic. Don't be that library. You can always showcase student work if you need visual interest. At the same time, I feel like there are a lot of libraries that go to the extreme, decorating every shelf with stuffed animals or dioramas. And too many libraries have dusty long-ago exemplars of student work showcased years after the student creators graduated. When student work on is display, it should be cycled in and out, being "on exhibit" rather than a fixture.

Writing about public libraries, Jordan (2014) asserts

> depressing surroundings, shabby furniture and materials, and dirty work environments do nothing to inspire librarians to work hard and provide the best service. A workplace consistently too hot or too cold, paint peeling from the walls, pieces of ceiling falling onto desks, with bugs and/or rodents infesting it all distract from the work of serving a community. These may not sound like important problems when compared to issues librarians face with decreasing budgets and increasing layoffs. But these seemingly small issues, faced every hour of every day and every week and every year spent at work, contribute to an overall elevated stress level. Stress caused by poor building conditions can lead to illness or even burnout for librarians condemned to work in substandard workplace facilities.

Not only are unattractive spaces miserable spaces to spend your working day, but they are unlikely to attract students. With effort and ingenuity, the library can be the most well-appointed place that many students will ever access.

One of the major challenges for learners today is the fact that there is so much instructional material everywhere they look. In many classes and in some libraries, Teachers-Pay-Teachers-sourced decorations have come to dominate every spare inch of the space. It can be impossible to establish focus in that sort of setting. While I'm a big fan of displays and know that libraries move books if they have them face out, I don't think you should "face" just any old book on the off chance it will attract a reader. Think of face-out books as your passive recommendation service and be choosy about what you include. A themed display and curated booklists focusing on the newest titles will pay dividends in terms of student engagement and eventual circulation. At all levels, it is appropriate to showcase a library's collection of books on particular themes and or highlight aspects of the collection. Not having materials on display is akin to saying you have nothing to share.

If the top of every single bookcase in the library is groaning with yellowing periodicals and things have found their way to the library out of a sort of preservationist instinct rather than whole-school significance, it might be time to find them other homes. That ubiquity of stuff can really create a lot of visual noise. I personally urge librarians to follow the lead of Marie Kondo, the Japanese woman who has made a tremendous international trend out of "the life-changing art of tidying up." You not only can but should discard the things that are no longer relevant or technologically supported in your school, that is part of your role as a professional. Outdated or unprocessed material objects can compound the anxieties that librarians have about their jobs. I have found administrators to be very supportive of paring back objects to the best of the best. This can lead to clarity of thought and an opportunity for overstimulated students to be calmed.

Too often librarians are cobbling together furniture from a variety of settings, and I have seen many not investing in computer furniture, citing the rate of change in technology. Today, furniture is relatively inexpensive, demanding less of an investment to redecorate, and modern pieces can provide integrated wired or even wireless charging, as well as providing integrated cable management systems that make the entire space tidier, and the technology more secure.

It's much less likely that your cords will disappear, or even become detached if they're properly managed with the appropriate furniture and zip or Velcro ties are a good investment.

Schools in general and school libraries in particular have moved away from static, institutional furniture toward more casual and variable seating arrangements which give the students more autonomy over their physical space. Standard tables have been supplanted as the learning commons trend has brought more multiuse furniture into play, with high and low seating and work surfaces suitable to active learning and variable grouping. Furniture should be mobile enough so it can be quickly redeployed either in small groups or in classrooms or theater settings. If you have comfortable seating like upholstered benches, couches, or armchairs, students will invariably come in just to sit, though with horizontally oriented furniture, you might want to check sightlines to ensure supervision.

ENGAGE ALL THE SENSES

When you think about what you want your space to be, do so with all your senses. Be ruthless about discarding musty and moldy materials. Consider a diffuser and essential oils to add scent to the space, and plug-in air fresheners go a long way to offset the stale air in study rooms. Is there music in your dream space? Is it ambient or classical or something more up-tempo? And don't forget about the ability to make changes through the inexpensive medium of paint. It can be a key part of achieving an updated look without expending a lot of money on decorating. For young learners especially, provide textures as means of sensation, be that carpet squares, pillows or beanbags. Smooth rocks and Montessori-style sandpaper letters offer other tactile experiences for those students that want to feel everything.

One trend in contemporary libraries seems to be bringing the outside in. More and more therapists are prescribing time in nature as a remedy for the ills of modern life and blurring the inside/outside lines can be soothing for you as well as your students. If you have a green thumb, this could be accomplished via potted plants or cut flowers, and rock gardens and freestanding fountains are low maintenance. By bringing in whatever is in bloom, be it tulips, daffodils or forsythia, you're creating a talking point as well as well alluding to the changing seasons.

What color is your library? This is not a question about the racial makeup of your collection development but rather a question about the environment. Are the colors calming? Are they exciting? An environment of pastel colors can be soothing for stressed-out teens, but an environment for younger children might be more stimulating. Alternating colors can help with directions ("the first shelf by the green wall") and creating a space for innervating activity as well as relaxation.

Perhaps the environmental factor that the librarian has the least control over is temperature. Climate control can be an either-or proposition, meaning you will be hot or cold and never comfortable. Computerized heating, ventilation, and air-conditioning (HVAC) settings are sometimes controlled centrally by a distant administrator at a central office, sometimes predetermined so that heating or cooling won't be on before a certain calendar date, despite the actual weather. Variations in heating and cooling can be detrimental to books. If you tend to run cold and bump up the thermostat, that warmth can have deleterious effects on learning. Think of how drowsy warm rooms can make you. Temperature is important because "heat lowers a child's ability to learn, according to an examination of 10 million American students that shows hotter school days reduce standardized test scores. Based on the analysis, every 1-degree-Fahrenheit increase in average outdoor temperature over a school year reduces student learning by 1 percent" (Akpan 2019). That study involved Preliminary Scholastic Apptitude Test (PSAT) scores for 10 million students who took the exam at least twice between 1998 and 2012, and compared those test scores to daily data from 3,000 weather stations for the same time period, as well as data on local pollution and economic conditions. The implications for global warming are real: "If we have two degrees of warming without any changes in infrastructure, then the implication is that the average student in the United States would learn around 7 percent less than he or she otherwise would have" (Akpan 2019). This is a scary prospect given changing climate; corresponding shifts in climate control within buildings, especially in older buildings without energy efficient modifications, could increase power costs significantly.

TECHNOLOGY ADJUSTMENTS

If you have a standing desk or bar-height, it can be purposed for an online public access catalog (OPAC) search station or for quick access for email or printing. Providing a charging station for student electronics will guarantee foot traffic. In many 1:1 settings with access to electronic resources, door count may be a more reliable indicator of library usage than circulation statistics. In my experience, the more students are in and out of the space, the more they will be disposed to ask for assistance when they need it, take you up on your materials recommendations, and just generally behave. If students are comfortable enough to lounge about in the library, you will have succeeded in creating a positive atmosphere which is important in creating the sort of environment that supports informal as well as formal learning.

As we consider what is necessary in library spaces in this day and age, it's hard to imagine a library space where there's not some sort of electronic projection available. Most instruction now involves a viewing experience, be it online demonstration, presentation software or video. Your projector might be mounted from a ceiling, but ideally you should have access to inputs and support hot swappable functionality so students or visitors to the library can share their own electronic work. If you're in a one-to-one computing environment, and students are issued Chromebooks or other types of laptops or iPads, your library technology should reflect that and be compatible so that students can work collaboratively on a larger screen instead of huddling over a single device. Don't forget that you can showcase students' electronic work, too.

Whatever your space, take responsibility for the way it looks as you take responsibility for the learning that takes place there. Never feel as if you must accept its shortcomings. Read articles showcasing innovative design in libraries of all types, visit as many as you can for inspiration, and as much as possible, pare down the unnecessary furniture and outdated materials and technology. Your library should be aspirational and a place of comfort and stimulation. It should also change to reflect the calendar and your student population. The best school libraries are the most dynamic.

REFERENCES

Akpan, Nsikan. 2019. "The Hotter the Planet Grows, the Less Children Are Learning." *PBS Newshour.* September 5, 2019. https://www.pbs.org/newshour/science/kids-learn-less-on-hot-days-global-warming-is-making-it-worse.

Jordan, Mary Wilkins. 2014. "All Stressed Out, But Does Anyone Notice? Stressors Affecting Public Libraries." *Journal of Library Administration* 54, no. 4 (May): 291–307. https://doi.org/10.1080/01930826.2014.924318.

Oldenburg, Ray. 2000. *Celebrating the Third Place: Inspiring Stories about the "Great Good Places" at the Heart of Our Communities.* Boston, MA: DeCapo.

THREE

Real Accessibility

Is it really a library if no one can use it? One of the things that was critical to meet the expressed needs of our high school students in our newly constructed space was the ongoing accessibility of the library before and after school. This was something that the students had raised in interviews with the principal and the paraprofessional, and I worked out a schedule with the school administration so that I would come in early 30 minutes before the campus officially opened so that the library would be accessible beginning at seven o'clock each morning. This was important to me because almost every day when I came to school I saw students waiting outside, and it seemed to me they could make more productive use of their time, though officially they had been forbidden access to campus until 7:30 a.m., but clusters of early birds simply stood near the doors waiting for us to open. My crackerjack paraprofessional assistant, who was a former public library director and had an MLIS of her own, volunteered to come in later, at ten o'clock, which left me working alone for those three hours in the morning. She would then stay until five o'clock in the afternoon, and I would be able to leave a little bit before three o'clock, a half an hour adjustment from the end of the contract day.

This was a case where our administrator was very responsive to what students wanted from the school and had the latitude to align support with these priorities. He could easily have chosen not to allow students to linger on campus after hours. There was a public library just a few blocks away, and there were a number of other public places with Wi-Fi access where students could work, but in approving this adjustment to staffing and scheduling, our principal was really realizing the value that we brought to both school library experience and the overall educational experience.

I cannot be enthusiastic about coffee shops in libraries, especially school libraries. The library is one of the last public places where there's no commercial imperative. Public school students should have some access to a democratic environment where they are not expected to make a purchase to participate in this space, unlike coffeehouse environments. By selling drinks even at nominal cost, we're creating a barrier for many students who will feel their inability to participate in that consumer interaction sharply. Removing any commercial aspect from your library—be it collecting money for fines or taking money for photocopies or printouts—changes the power dynamic to make the space necessarily more inclusive. I had an administrator reiterate the idea that for many students, the school building will be the nicest place they will ever be. Be sure that remains associated with intellectual rather than commercial provision.

LIMINALITY AND THE LIBRARY AS LIMINAL SPACE

It is important to openly define the purpose of the space because for many students, the school library may be the first library they have experienced. One of my colleagues at Jacksonville State University introduced me to the concept of liminal spaces and it forever changed my perspective on how many students experience libraries. Melanie Wallace teaches counseling. She is interested in how an individual is moving into a new space, which is not one that they have known before, such as when they approach a counselor. That unfamiliarity of the space, its uncertainty, and the lack of definition of the counseling relationship all contribute to the dialogue that emerges between the counselor and the counseled. I began to notice associated concepts recurring in conversations about public and private spaces.

The concept of liminality came from sociologist Bruno Latour's studies of tribes (2005, 4–8). He observed that in some communities, young boys went away from home for a while and then were considered to be men when they returned. While they were away, there was this in-between period where they were on their own, without familiarity or signposts of identity.

Liminality definitely applies within school libraries in particular. Students are perhaps more accustomed to being in a classroom or a cafeteria or gymnasium. Visits to the library may be less certain, especially for students in older grades who are not on fixed library schedules. The etymology of *liminal* borrows from the Latin and evokes thresholds. Libraries should be a literal threshold to a universe of information but also sort of a virtual threshold to a place where you can define yourself in different ways and try different types of information sources.

Try to walk into your space with a beginner's mind. Do you feel like livestock being herded in an abattoir? Too often libraries constrain traffic by funneling students through narrow passages. Architecture critic Aaron Betsky calls for the creation of more "empty rooms," "an architecture that does not delineate public and private space, does not articulate the common, and does not connect us in a prescribed manner. I would argue for a leaky, confusing, difficult to understand and perhaps even to use architecture that, somehow, somewhere and maybe even sometimes, creates the sense that we are only truly alive when we are part of a social construct in which we can act out the roles we believe or are proper to us" (Betsky 2015). It is a thoughtful way to describe the stage set for intellectual activity that is a school library, where students often come, uncertain of what they want to take away, be it materials for reading, sources for research, or merely the experience of having time away from the more predictable environment of the classroom.

A secondary definition of liminality is characterized by being on a boundary or on a threshold, that of an "in-between state." That too is true for school libraries, as students move in and out of them. For some students, the library may even be an avenue used to get from class to class. Something that can exacerbate this threshold sensation is the monolithic circulation desk that is installed in so many school libraries. Sometimes, the desk may be positioned like that in a bank, almost as if it is a safety concern with you being approached. Large desks might seem necessary to accommodate materials for the piecemeal desk work librarians always have to do, but I think it is better to be visible in the library. As one of my library school professors stressed, librarians must balance being accessible and getting work done. Librarians should always be interruptible, and a staff desk that looms over the students does not welcome questions. By positioning the student in the role of supplicant, they reinforce this barrier rather than the connection. Oftentimes, the circulation desk is both wide *and* high. In my opinion, the only thing worse than a librarian seemingly stranded behind a desk is the librarian out of sight in the office. A lower desk is more welcoming and pulls in the student. I love the idea of students actually sitting across from the librarian or side by side at the circulation desk during reference interviews and other transactions, with monitors that pivot so that you can share what you're looking at and that students can share what they're looking at with you. Being able to share your search process and results in this way will reinforce the metacognitive aspects of information literacy while at the same time helping to alleviate the asymmetrical power dynamics inherent in the school setting.

If the desk, like a dinner table, is communal, a librarian, a paraprofessional aide, student helpers, and students needing support can all work collectively. Sharing space emphasizes that you are a part of a learning community. Accessibility should include the ability to create space for ongoing, just-in-time consultations as needed rather than appearing like deus ex machina from a remote office. We all know the uncertain feeling of walking into a seemingly empty library. By positioning yourself more centrally, you will be in place to welcome students and teachers and associate the space with helpful service provision.

Like the empty library, examples of physically liminal spaces include the sense of being in the middle of the wilderness without signposts or being in a place that was formerly inhabited and now isn't. Think of an abandoned shopping mall or an airport gate after the last flights, places where one cannot be hundred percent confident, safe or secure. In the literature around liminality and counseling, a lot of psychologists have stressed that the process of preparation for a counseling degree requires being in constant flux. Students like definitive answers and routines and, until older adolescence, can demand certitude. Only in early adulthood do people become more comfortable with ambiguity. It's something that I try to stress with graduate students, because hopefully by that point in their professional career they have embraced ambiguity as something that is inherent as well as part of the part and parcel of daily life. But that doesn't mean we shouldn't acknowledge how that uncertainty feels for young people, anticipate issues, and try to ameliorate them.

THE INFORMATION SEARCH PROCESS AND THE EXPECTATION OF UNCERTAINTY

If we're talking about confusion and ambiguity, there is no better expression of uncertainty in school libraries than Carol Kuhlthau's seminal model. Developed for her dissertation research, it has since been adopted as applicable in almost every information literacy setting (1991). Kuhlthau focused on the affective, and in doing that, opened a new paradigm in information literacy by recognizing that the emotions that the searcher was experiencing were both affecting the research process and were predictable. The transitory and cyclic nature of the Information Search Process (ISP) model emphasizes that those temporary feelings of anxiety will resolve as students found the pertinent information, revised their research question, and began to make sense of that information that they had collected, and it emphasizes the zone of intervention for the librarian. The ISP confirms the sensations of uncertainty associated with liminality and provides another way to appreciate the affective experience of students in the library space.

WHERE DOES THIS FIT INTO THE AASL STANDARDS?

Regarding liminal spaces, Land, Rattray, and Vivian (2014) wrote, "Certain concepts and practices are forms of learning experience can act in the manner of a portal or learning threshold through a new perspective opens for the learner the latter enters new conceptual terrain in which things formally not perceived coming to view this permits new and previously inaccessible ways to thinking in practice." Libraries should aspire to connect learners with information in this same way. That, and not merely possessing an Internet-connected device, is real accessibility for learners.

Looking at the 2017 Iteration of American Association of School Librarians (AASL)'s Standards for Learners, you will find verbiage about demonstrating an understanding of and a commitment to inclusiveness and respect for diversity within the learning community. A congruent aspect with the AASL Standards would be the grow feature associated with the *Include* standard, with "learners demonstrating empathy and equity and knowledge building." The library is a space for learners to practice exhibiting empathy, tolerance for diverse ideas, and space for discussions with those multiple viewpoints. Creating and maintaining an inclusive and accessible library space will enable you to do that sort of standards work in your library. To accomplish that, students must have interactions with a range of learners of different ages and levels. In a library space, not only can students develop their own beliefs but appreciate other perspectives, a skill that will serve them well in any future.

REFERENCES

American Association of School Librarians (AASL). 2017. "Standards Framework for Learners." https://standards.aasl.org/wp-content /uploads/2017/11/AASL-Standards-Framework-for-Learners -pamphlet.pdf.

Betsky, Aaron. 2015. "Beyond Buildings: Empty Halls Mean Freedom?" *Architect Magazine*. June 13, 2018. https://www.architectmagazine .com/design/empty-halls-mean-freedom_o.

Kuhlthau, C. C. 1991. "Inside the Search Process: Information Seeking from the User's Perspective." *Journal of the American Society for Information Science* 42, no. 5: 361–371.

Land, R., J. Rattray, J., and P. Vivian. 2014. "Learning in the Liminal Space: A Semiotic Approach to Threshold Concepts." *Higher Education* 67, no. 2: 199–217.

Latour, Bruno. 2005. *Reassembling the Social: An Introduction to Actor-Network Theory.* Oxford, UK: Oxford UP.

FOUR

Procedures and Policies for Positive Interactions

The easiest way to promote mindfulness through your school library space might be as simple as adjusting your circulation policies. Are they outdated? We live in an age of material abundance, and that includes books. This should allow us as school librarians to hone our collections until they provide the very best for our readers, but it should also signal a shift in priorities, away from the material to the personal. I would argue that it is no longer necessary to restrict borrowing unnecessarily and assign punitive fines and block students' future access for failure to return materials on time. There will always be egregious cases, where students want to blithely take out dozens of books, many more than they can possibly keep up with, or fail to return the most popular materials other readers are waiting for in rapt anticipation, and these can be dealt with on a case-by-case basis rather than applying limitations across the board. For so many readers and materials, our twentieth-century circulation policies might be overkill. Figure out how you can make these promote reading and accessibility rather than situating the librarian as a policeman for collections.

WHY QUIET STUDY IS STILL RELEVANT

We have far fewer silent school libraries than in the past. Many libraries today celebrate the fact that they are noisy, populated environments. While this is a terrific demonstration of the vitality of the learning community in these schools and spaces, as far as individual students' needs go, it is important to recognize that not all learners will have access to quiet spaces to concentrate at home. Many students will have learning differences that require more focused attention. By setting aside areas of your library for quiet study, you are reinforcing the validity of the learning style represented by learners who engage with text on the page rather than learning in co-constructed social situations. Ideally, school libraries should balance both sorts of spaces, so figure out some way to negotiate the need for both types of environments for your students.

If your library tends to be a high-energy place, create a "calming area" using bookshelves or other partitions to symbolize a shift in mood and tone. High levels of stimulation can make it difficult for many learners to focus. Sensitive or traumatized children are not always able to recognize or articulate when they are feeling overwhelmed. By making a space in your library that is accessible when students feel stressed, anxious, or vulnerable, you can provide them with ongoing opportunities to identify emotions and an accessible strategy to better regulate them.

Most schools, and many libraries, have areas that are flashpoints for student conflict. These may be just out of your sight line, or outside the doors to the space, or in stairwells, if you have those. Make monitoring those areas, especially during transitions, a regular part of your routine. I remember capturing some videos for another purpose and realizing that a corner of the library was almost entirely blind from my usual vantage point. First and foremost, we need to ensure student safety, and that can include heading off assignations as well as conflicts. Physical and psychological safety should be a cornerstone of a mindful, student-centered school environment.

TEACHING REFLECTION IN SMALL STEPS

I'm a big believer in the practice of journaling and will talk more about this in the next chapter. Training students to capture thoughts and feelings on paper or via text or drawing in a reflective manner will help them be less reactive in the moment. Many disciplines use notebooks and research notes across projects and topics. Getting students into the habit of keeping either digital or paper-based commonplace books as they encounter information with access points for future information is a critical life skill. Bullet journaling is very trendy at the moment, and programming around that, as delivered by Lance Simpson at the Tuscaloosa Public

Library, can help refine the capture-input-reflect cycle of digital-age projects.

I also believe that short pieces of literature can have wonderful effects in terms of improving mental health. One easy way libraries can support interpersonal intellectual conversation and appreciation is the promotion of *short reading*, one of the trends identified by ALA's Center for the Future of Libraries. Think of the short poems used as public service announcements on mass transit. In posting either short stories or poems in publicly accessible places for student consumption, you can draw in their attention and feed their souls. You can always encourage reader response through reflection as well, by posting a provocative question and supplying Post-it notes or other materials for students to respond on a whiteboard or chalkboard.

This is one small step to make your school library space feel more interactive and involve students. Almost all young people enjoy quick and creative activities that allowed them to express their personalities and feelings. Collective spaces like libraries are the perfect place to establish community and reflect the mosaic of differences that exist within our schools. I believe crowdsourcing student knowledge can be an easy first step for establishing a safe space for sharing among the learning community. Existing bulletin boards or white boards can be provided with prompts to solicit student feedback, and most of them will take a moment when offered to write and draw with supplied markers. Before Valentine's Day, you might ask students who their "book crush" might be, then arrange books with those characters nearby. For Banned Websites Awareness Day, you could ask secondary students which sites they wish that they had access to on the school network and why.

One easy way to create a high-traffic, useful, and inclusive space involves using technology to shift the scene. I would advise any library to include a green screen station, which can be little more than a wall, either painted green or using an inexpensive green felt cloth for a backdrop— dollar store tablecloths of the appropriate color can be substituted in a pinch, and a tablet on a tripod with green screen apps installed. I have one student whose action research for her EdS involved tracking the use of her makerspace, and she discovered that two-thirds of the traffic there involved using the green screen. The green screen uses the same chromakey technology that allows meteorologists to be visible in front of the electronic weather maps projected behind them; it can be easily accomplished using a range of free applications that provide the ability to situate foregrounded objects in front of digital images or videos. Creative uses range from layering student to appear in front of distant locales to allowing an illusion of performance in front of elaborate stage sets. In this middle school library, the green screen was a huge draw, despite much more considerable expenditures on robotics and other equipment. Green screen technology also has the advantage of inculcating very important information literacy lessons about the appearance of presence that informs everything from movie making to computer-generated "deep fake" construction. Students with hands-on experience of the verisimilitude allowed by this sort of technological layering will be much savvier about videos they encounter.

WHAT DOES A MINDFUL SCHOOL LIBRARY COLLECTION LOOK LIKE?

It goes without saying that collection considerations will vary greatly based on your school community readers and teachers. Being responsive to local community needs is important and will help situate the library at the heart of the school. Much of this will depend on the curriculum in your building, the projects that teachers return to each year, and the availability of resources through other local libraries. The curriculum should be evident in the collection. In lean budget times, I know that I only purchased nonfiction related to recurring school assignments. I felt it was better to spend limited funds on the materials that would be used rather than trying to anticipate or forecast student interest or try to round out the collection based on a platonic ideal of what a library should hold. While I do believe that there is such a thing as a core collection I also believe that the scale of what can be considered a core collection is shrinking smaller and smaller every year as digital information sources replaces print and access supplants ownership.

Your library probably provides a range of information that, while not strictly part of the collection, contributes to the overall educational mission of the library within the school. And much of that may be of local interest and import. If you are dropped, blindfolded, in a distant point, you should immediately be able to tell where you are by looking around the library. This is low-hanging fruit in terms of making your space both more appealing and more student centered. Local history and geography areas are two of the things all school libraries tend to excel in, so why not showcase these little-digitized resources to share the value of a range of materials with the students and teachers in your building? If the materials are out of copyright, you might consider a digitization project, either independently or as part of a local, state, or regional initiative. These are ways you can add lasting value to the profession and community.

It goes without saying that acquisitions should be patron-driven and there should be multiple mechanisms for students to request books beyond them asking you for them in face-to-face interactions. Online forms linked from the library catalog, a shoebox in a corner, a focus group of your advisory board can all supply suggestions for desired materials students will really read. An important consideration in your collection development is understanding the changing nature of literacies and not reinforcing outdated ideas about formats like cartoons and comics. I would advise against demonizing any content wholesale, realizing that art and entertainment exists in many forms. Too many school librarians avoid age-appropriate, high-interest materials because of the potential for challenges, many of which occur from within the school. Many librarians I know have grappled with these sorts of concerns, like the first-year teacher who wanted to punish a student for consuming materials they felt were inappropriate during independent reading. Anyone who is an avid reader themselves will realize the folly of demanding every book in the library be morally edifying; reading practice is what is important, and the same faculty who would never cast aspersions on a student's untoward dietary or sartorial choices will take up the mantle when it concerns intellectual content. I remember a high school librarian I was assigned to mentor who called in a panic because a substitute teacher had confiscated a library copy of James Patterson's *The Affair*, and the complaint seemed grounded in the cover art. But the students loved James Patterson, she insisted. I knew she was right and that this was a disciplinary issue rather than an intellectual freedom one. As another veteran librarian advised, keep the book off the shelf for a bit but then return it.

Among the most difficult thing to do in the library can be acknowledging the concerns of other faculty and administration while also championing intellectual freedom. I worked with another high school librarian who rejected any form of profanity in books, deeming the award-winning Hazelwood High trilogy by Sharon Draper "trash." Her purchases were almost entirely series nonfiction to support curricular research projects. I did understand where she was coming from. She had been through a high-profile materials challenge where the complaint was covered by the local television news. But her school struggled with test scores in reading, and for me it seemed a natural outgrowth of having nothing any student would want to read in the library.

I have found that school librarians who know their collections and their community tend to have fewer reservations about content. Given the variety of explicit information available online, I hope that school librarians will realize that students are exposed to much more than the occasional four-letter word or dysfunctional family set-up. That is not to say that you do not need to choose the very best books for your patron group, and that includes discarding things with outdated messages and images. New school librarians have a challenge in becoming familiar with a collection they did not choose. And sometimes books are ordered and make it into the collection through mistake; I remember walking around a K–6 library as an administrative intern, pulling out several books with explicit young adult (YA) content that had obviously been ordered because their titles contained elementary-sounding concepts. After all, we are rightly subject to the expectation that we will know our collections intimately. I believe that, by reading a little every day, we can accomplish this over time, and if we don't have that time to read, we do not have the time to be librarians. It is part of our professional responsibility.

Another way to build an inclusive and an emotionally supportive library collections includes having picture books to use with students of all ages. We push too many readers past picture books in an attempt to build reading ability and stamina; too many children enter school already being discouraged from the wonderful world of illustrations. And for older readers, picture books can serve to activate prior knowledge, create empathy, and present curricular standards in succinct digestible and pithy ways. You may need to work with your faculty on using picture books, because too many will want to rush through them without consideration of art to support the narrative. By slowing down and spending time on text, you're emphasizing that they are examining works of art, and sharing the really carefully considered construction of images in picture books. Reading a range of materials in class does create community and creates a sort of new type of literacy. Fortunately, more and more teachers are realizing that excellent trade picture books are a tool for students of all ages, including college and graduate students.

RESTRUCTURING DISCIPLINE

The library should take a note from classroom-based discipline philosophies that empower the teacher to take action without loss of instructional time. The library should not be subject to different sorts of considerations, and your administration will appreciate your being proactive in working to correct student behavior in the space rather than delegating this responsibility to someone else.

One of the easiest feelings to pinpoint and perhaps the easiest to address with young people is that of anger. This is one area where bibliotherapeutic approaches can be particularly helpful with younger students. But there are myriad ways of releasing negative emotions. Think about ways that you as a school librarian can facilitate anger management as a cultural practice. Schools that have had success with social emotional learning plan regular times for sharing feelings, whether this is using a systematic approach like a mood meter, a one-on-one check in with an adviser, or more future-focused exploration. Is there a way to formalize the sharing circles that are already going on in your school library space? If students feel comfortable sharing their feelings and talking to each other about what makes them angry it will go a long way to diffusing tensions.

Physical activity is another simple, no-cost tool that can be used to channel negative energies. Even if it's not high impact exercise, moving from one space to another can do much to offer everyone a different perspective. By the time many students come to your space, they may have let go of the anger they experienced elsewhere. If not, giving them a minute to sit quietly can work wonders, and if it is a "special space" like the library office, it might be doubly distracting. Every librarian knows kids that benefit from shifts in surroundings during the school day. The need for motion might be formally attributed to hyperactivity or oversensitivity or a flight response, but make sure your teachers know that the school library will always provide safe harbor for these students. Having a school culture that respects the need for time for mood regulation—whether you call it taking a break, a timeout, a cool down, or a change of scene—supports all students' needs.

When students can't expel nervous energy through motion, journaling can be a terrific tool for letting go of negative thoughts. There seem to be two types of journalers: those who choose to revisit their thoughts and those who could just as easily discard they're writing never see it again. Outcomes-oriented students may want to know, is it about the product or the process? With journaling, it's both. While gathering information for this project, I discovered a list from last year among my journals. It was a series of things I had aspired to in 2018—conference presentations, journal submissions, organization elections—that been denied, rejected, or just not picked. Looking at the precise and enumerated list a year later, I hardly remembered many of the items I had outlined, and I realized that the exercise had more than served its purpose, enabling me to move on and focus on new opportunities. This year, I attempted and failed at just as many things, and I can't remember being as upset as this detailed list from last year signals that I was then. By creating this list, I had thought that I was documenting my many deficiencies, but it ended up giving me permission to fail and also not to dwell on those failures.

GROUP DYNAMICS

Consider how the school library can create groups that promote inclusivity, especially for students who might not be part of other student organizations. At one school where I worked, someone noticed that academically struggling students were less likely to be involved in student activities. Though correlation does not equal causation, the administration announced that everyone was going to have to join an organization. The goal was for 100 percent participation in extracurricular activities. While I understood the impulse, I have a knee-jerk reaction to any sort of mandate. Surely not everyone would want to participate? But students seem to find possibilities in the directive and checked boxes for existing groups or even went so far as to originate new groups in their areas of interest. All of us, even the loners sitting by themselves in the corner, need to feel we belong. Don't set expectations for a number of students required for a group, because this can exclude some of the students with the most passionate interests. Combining those with niche interests into umbrella groups can be structured to allow the students the autonomy of their own concerns while promoting dialogue between those of different affinities.

How to Hack Time

There are so many things we want to do in our spaces, and we want to intimately know our students and our collections, but there may seem to be finite time in the day. One of the most critical aspects to developing a mindful lifestyle is the ability to manage time in an effective and efficient way. Perhaps the most personally influential jobs that I ever had outside librarianship was working in television production in the mid-1990s. That was an experience that fundamentally changed my thinking about the whole setup of time and work. Television production was such that you worked toward the show in a very relaxed and seemingly haphazard way for several hours, and then you had a very intense experience while you were on the air for a half hour or an hour. There were several things that were sort of consequences of the nature of live local television. One of those was that you learned to be competent at your task. If you were not competent, you would not last in the pressure-cooker on-air periods. Being live demanded that, within the span of sometimes five seconds, you had to be able to change the focus of a camera or amend a graphic. The nature of production was such that you had to be able to do a variety of tasks very quickly while also anticipating a range of issues that were likely to arise. This was such a high-stakes environment that there was actually a report generated after every broadcast that listed "discrepancies" from the production scripts that were generated before the broadcast. It was a very bad thing to appear on this disseminated discrepancy list as having made a mistake.

Working in television really changed my attitude entirely about the sorts of things that I could get done in a very brief amount of time, and this is something that has carried into every other job I've had since then. I have always known that 30 seconds is a wealth of time to send an email, to research a topic to assist a student, or to embrace a teachable moment to show someone an information literacy skill. Time management is a fundamental disposition that made me very susceptible to ideas emerging around productivity, many of them having spun off from a sort of tech-adjacent lifestyle hacking zeitgeist.

It is entirely possible to hack time. This will be something that I will return to again and again, because I do feel like it is an essential tool for developing a mindful existence. Finite time, and panic around that, is one of the greatest enemies of flow. I believe one of the tragedies of modern technologies is the inability to expedite processes because we as users are monetized based on the amount of our attention that can be captured. Theoretically technology should make everything easier, but oftentimes we end up digitizing things that would be much more efficiently accomplished with analog tools. But there are a lot of ways to automate tasks that drain the new commodities of your energy and attention as well as your time.

One tool I find fascinating is the "hipster PDA (personal digital assistant)." But it is far from digital, instead cutting down a blank index card until it is a quarter or eighth the size of a three-by-five index card. These minicards can be held together using a binder clip, which in turn can be rigged to fit onto a keychain. The genius of the hipster PDA is enabling, through tiny bits of cardstock, notetaking. Or if you need to provide some-one with information in a written format, you can give them a note scrib-bled on one. It is a way to ensure that you always have what David Allen (2002) calls a "container" to capture information as it occurs to you. That might be a book recommendation, holiday hours, a website to visit, or a list of tasks to complete. The idea is that as you get those things into a sys-tem, you will get them out of your mind. In capturing the information in note format, you are effectively creating an appointment to be sure to add to another container or calendar. But this first step demands you need to have a container accessible at all times.

GETTING THINGS DONE

David Allen has been called "the Henry Ford of the digital age," and if you were to sum up his system in one in one sentence, it would be get things out of your head and into a trusted system. His book *Getting Things Done: The Art of Stress-Free Productivity* (2002) and systems are based upon the idea that all the inputs that you collect on a daily basis either rep-resent an action that needs to be done or a project that is an umbrella for a group of actions. Allen estimates he has to make between 300 and 400 decisions to sort inputs every day; he believes that you should deal with things that you can deal with within a very short window of time at the moment they occur. Allen's philosophy goes back to my experience at the television studio where I discovered that you could achieve results in very short amounts of time. Allen and his many devotees offer suggestions for streamlining the system, things like checking your email inbox with your finger on the delete key. A system of folders can store necessary informa-tion for access later, but it's likely you're able to clear 90 percent of what you encounter without that affecting your attention. The beauty of Allen's system is that you limit what enters your consciousness. You can adopt aspects of Getting Things Done to add appointments and reminders to your always-open calendar. Most email can be sorted into things that can be responded to quickly—a request to have a class visit the library, notifi-cation that a student might be on their way, responding to requests for simple directory types of information—all of these can be dealt with immediately and without causing you mental strain.

Allen stresses that you should decide on what will become of material items immediately, and there is no place where this is more true than in the library. Oftentimes, libraries will be sent things; we're not sure what to do with them, and we'll just stick them in a corner or leave them in the box or bag or whatever they came in because someone at some point in some distant unknown time in some distant unknown future may want them.

Instead of storing things that are of no immediate applicability, create a cooperative space within your library or even better your teacher workroom, away from the library, where instructional materials can be shared for those who want them, and then schedule and promote a regular clear out of some of those areas. It is true that we never know what other people might find useful, but some people are loath to discard anything. This is why the subject of weeding is a tremendous hot potato in so many schools; there will be some teachers who hate to see any books discarded and they will take materials that have been deaccessioned into their classroom regardless of whether or not those were up-to-date, factual, attractive to students, or entirely superseded.

Every school librarian I know has a story of a teacher rescuing something that they had discarded and what they're not realizing is that the library is a growing organism, as Ranganathan told us, and that libraries are not museums. As school teachers, so many of us are used to parsimony and saving everything that we come across that could have instructional value that we can forget that we live in a time of abundance, and there are more material goods than we know how to deal with. Free space is often more valuable to our psyche than the materials objects we fill it with, so we have the issue now of having to edit, discard, and evaluate every object to see if, as William Morris told us, it is beautiful or useful, and, if neither of those is true, we can consider whether or not it will continue to have a place in our libraries.

Allen says to review your lists and folders—the things that you have created as containers for your different tasks and projects—as often as required "to keep them out of your head." Your container and your files may be the same interface. I personally really like the IOS app Clear and use it to create lists of projects I'm working, on trips that I have coming up, and I can adapt and duplicate lists as required. Another valuable tool is Google Keep, a handy cloud-based notation device with browser plug-ins to allow you to save images as well as a variety of other types of media and annotate them. Saved Google Keep notes appear on a pinboard-type screen, and you can sort based on a number of criteria or choose to elevate to the top of a board. Also, if you never learned keyboard shortcuts using command keys, that is one thing I really recommend for efficiency, as is touch-typing, which can be easily accomplished on a particular machine by training using one of the silicon keyboard covers used for keyboarding classes. If you have worked in an environment where you had to use something like vi, an early text editor, you'll know how time-saving those types of commands and techniques can be when you're doing knowledge work like librarianship. Another strategy that can be helpful are the use of labels, be they text labels or colors, to sort tasks by kind.

I cannot emphasize enough how much Getting Things Done helps with mental acuity. I have not implemented the system with strict fidelity, but instead have adopted pieces that into my needs and lifestyle. After more than a decade of working the system, I am now able to function without any anxiety about a range of minutiae, appointments, and tasks. GTD is a cognitive shift unlike anything else I have undergone as an adult. Allen calls it "the mind like water," and there's something to that analogy. GTD facilitates "flow" and supports the ability to be creative when your attention is rested and not fragmented by the many routine and recurring details that occupy so much of our time and attention.

GETTING TO INBOX ZERO

One recurring theme in the productivity community is the idea of getting your email box "to zero." "Getting to zero" does not mean that you'll actually not have any email anywhere reflecting ongoing projects, but it means instead that everything will have been filed appropriately and responded to as necessary. There are a number of systems that have been evolved and popularized to help. A common one is moving things you will respond to at some point in the future into some sort of pending or follow-up file. If you don't sort this way, your inbox becomes your to-do list, and your tasks will be buried under other communications. In categorizing things appropriately, your inbox can still be at zero, which is a real psychic burden lifted.

I have found the best types of folders for me personally are either very specific ("AASL Louisville 2019" or "JSU Salary Study") with a designation that is for specific conference or for a specific student, rather than one that is general and amorphous like "technology" or "professional development"— it might be helpful to think of hashtags, and adjust themes periodically to be sure they best reflect their contents. In my own system, anything "pinned" to the top of a folder will remain divided out for reference, and anything "flagged" represents something ongoing. Those emails nested in this way in folders become your project-specific to do list. There are some things that might be useful in the future, but do not sort easily. These are the sort of things I would once bookmark using delicious or my browser, but now in each account I have a kind of a catch-all folder, which I call "interesting," and anything that I might want to consult later but that might not fit any of my established folders may go there. It could just be a link to a website that I've never heard of that I want to be sure to check out. I can visit this sort of holding pen of digital information that I want to remember exist but I don't have time to check out at the moment as time allows.

David Allen suggests email and file folders should represent themes, topics, or persons. He relies a lot on keyword searching of files, something I personally have found to be less productive. I tend to think that you know the things you will need to access again and again. If you develop the proper system of folders it is entirely possible to never leave a read email in your inbox, Just as you sort through your postal mail over a waste paper basket, scan your inbox with your finger on that delete key and make sure that you know especially how to sort efficiently in your mobile email interface if you have one, which is another choice that I think more people are making is decoupling communications to allow them more control over their own time and attention. If you choose to be accessible via mobile email, you should be able to sort your incoming emails into folders in a maximum of two steps. The necessity for this ruthless purging and organization becomes clearer when you really think about every message in your inbox as a psychic burden that is generating a tiny bit of stress in your mind. Emptying the inbox does not imply that the work is done, but just implies that you have taken an action.

You need to build time to maintain your email inbox into your schedule. The frequency that you will need to do that really depends upon the volume of communications also on the efficiency of your own processing. David Allen suggests twice a day can be adequate for most people, and I have many productivity-minded friends who are real converts to twice-a-day batch process of email. One is a professor who's very clear with his students that those are the times that he will respond to them. Through a communications policy on his syllabus, he has really established that as a norm for communication. Another batching devotee I know is in a corporate position, and he really praises the improvement in his work output after scheduling his email as he would conference call or any other type of entry on his calendar. I find that, especially in school environments where you are expected to communicate electronically throughout the day, this might not be realistic. For most of us, we'll have to monitor communications (be it through email, slack, or some other program) throughout the working day, even if that's just glancing at the email inbox subject lines and from fields between classes. You can use IFTTT (If This Then That, more in subsequent text) to ensure sure that messages from certain contacts are pushed through two mobile devices or your phone, creating an almost ambient awareness. As information professionals we're on the bleeding edge of information distribution, so our need to monitor our email inboxes is probably a little bit more stringent than many of our colleagues who have different types of instructional roles.

Now that most emails allow for almost-infinite storage, email requires more maintenance. The individual messages and larger, and the pace of e-lists has increased. The mere suggestion of unlimited memory is a curse because it enables you to think that you can save everything for future consultation. The fact of the matter is, if you save everything then what you do have becomes less valuable and less useful for you as a tool, though this may be less true if you are an adept user of the search feature built into your email programs. Nonetheless, because of untargeted keyword searching, I have found too many people struggle with retrieving email from these sorts of unlimited accounts. When I see badges with five- or six-digit numbers reflecting unread items on the email app on someone's smart phone, I shudder. Each of those emails is a psychic burden. Deal with it on the front end.

How many email addresses do you have? If you don't have different email accounts for commercial transactions and separate accounts for websites requiring registration, that is an easy way to slow the flow into your inbox. If you use Gmail, you can add a plus and then text to your email address before the @ sign—whatever is after your email address will become nested in its own folder.

The real benefit to systemizing information inputs is that it will have an unexpected effect by paradoxically allowing you to go longer without checking for new messages. Because you have responded to things as they have occurred, and they are no longer undone, you don't have that sensation of always being behind or having procrastinated, and you can get so many communications off your mind immediately.

CALENDARS

Many popular productivity tools force you to make a trade-off between privacy and efficiency. I put browser extensions, most of which harvest data, personalized browsers, search engines, and myriad cloud-based digital products in the category where every user must decide for themselves about their comfort level regarding personal information sharing and free digital tools. I have found using a Calendars App overlay to access Google Calendars, synced between devices, to be a life-changing process. I've been using my online calendar for more than a decade, and I relished the ability to go back and see when I did particular things at particular times. It has made it very easy, for example to generate travel information for visa purposes. I color code my calendars, with one for personal appointments, travel, and reminders, another for professional obligations, and a third for work obligations. When working on short-term projects such as this book, I have developed specific calendars for those tasks. Those can be toggled on and off and ultimately, deleted when they are no longer required. I appreciate the ability to schedule tasks weekly, monthly, and even annually, which is very handy when remembering people's birthdays. Recurring events can be set to repeat based on the day of the month or the day of the week, and you can build in an expiration at the end of the semester or year. If you delete a particular appointment from a recurring sequence, most calendars will ask whether you want to delete the entire sequence or series, and I find that very useful as well. Within Calendars, there is the ability to set reminders to send yourself a desktop or email notification. I use these judiciously when I do set them their incredibly helpful. Another approach I use rarely but for impact is color coding important due dates or deadlines with red or orange as they approach.

The collaborative aspects of many online calendars have been embraced by many schools and communities. The only downside I have seen is the proliferation of spam via online calendars; since you can add tasks via email, it is easy for people to spoof the necessary email address and add their own appointments to your calendar. Of course, any online information provides data points for marketers and has the potential to be monetized. This is doubly true when you're using a secondary tool like Calendars to access information hosted elsewhere. All users should do their due diligence when it comes to online tools and decide whether the particular privacy trade-off is worth it for them in each particular instance.

Wearable devices are another tool that, when used deliberately, can increase productivity and focus. If your texts are coming to your wrist you probably will not feel as compelled to monitor your telephone in case a babysitter or a friend has an emergency. The ability of newer devices to function on wireless networks without Bluetooth connection to a mobile phone has the potential to slow our distractions to a trickle and revolutionize ambient awareness.

If This Then That (IFTTT) is a linking service that allows you to establish conditions where if one thing happens, another thing will happen automatically via automation. It works through accessing your data to create a sequence of events, essentially programming how you want that information to come to you. One example would be text reminders for all of your Google Calendar events, something that is no longer supported within Google Calendar itself. You can go into IFTTT and set that up as a "recipe"; "recipe" represents any series of events to happen sequentially. IFTTT works with most of the major online interfaces. Some ingenious uses for this tool include blogging the amount of time that you spend in specific places based on location information and getting an email reminder a week before your wedding anniversary. You can automatically back up texts from an Android device to a Google spreadsheet, something that might be potentially useful for parents. My only concern is that IFTT requires access to your accounts to work, and always remember that personal data has become among your most precious commodities, at least as far as technology corporations go.

One of the analogies that occurs with the Getting Things Done productivity community is that of "the runway" of your current actions. Everything that you're doing at the moment should lead toward the advancement of your projects, its liftoff, and those are going to reflect your areas of responsibility. So, broadly thinking, you will have ongoing projects (whether or not you have recognized them as such) in your career, in your personal life, and for professional development. As you get a broader perspective on each of those areas, you're better able to plan for where you want to be in the future, with the ultimate goal being cruising altitude for long-term stability. Achieving life goals will always be represented as having this forward and upward motion in mind, so it is easy to ensure that your current tasks and actions and projects are feeding into this larger goal.

Hacking time is a process that every user must work out for themselves and develop the sorts of approaches and methods for processing information that makes sense based on the influx in their own lives. But when things are successfully systematized, they do free you up, and if you're freed up for sufficiently long, in time, you can experience that "mind like water" that Allen described, perhaps as close to a state of sustained flow as most contemporary humans will experience. Best of all, freeing yourself up in this way will make it easier to be empathetic and to focus on inter-actions with students and teachers in the relationships that are at the crux of school library practice.

REFERENCE

Allen, David. 2002. *Getting Things Done: The Art of Stress-Free Productivity.* New York: Penguin.

FIVE

Slowing Down Research

For the purposes of this book, mindfulness can be considered as intentionality. Myriad examples of embracing mindfulness tend to be associated with moments of change—changes in method of instruction, staffing, hours, or collections. We all know how disruptive change can be when it is merely for the sake of change. Too often, change is used as a form of signaling. In your school library context, perhaps it's finally allowing students to eat lunch in the library, planning gaming events when gaming was previously banned, or investing in new formats or genres that would have been anathema to an earlier regime or to support new hardware. After all, the urge to embrace and promote novelty can be irresistible. But beyond reaction or filling gaps, and beyond signifying that we *once did that, but now we no longer will*, are you meeting the needs of students and teachers? Too often, we are moving too fast to tell.

We all know that the need for reflection is a common refrain in the world of education. I consider intentionality to be building upon informed reflective practice. Reflection in school settings can become part of the furniture—I know I probably did not appreciate how our profession had integrated reflective analysis as a summative activity until I began working with faculty from other disciplines at the university level. Several of my colleagues in other fields cited the importance of being taught post-facto reflection, usually in the context of having taken an education course. Collecting teaching evaluations, exit slips, or postproduct feedback may seem old hat to teachers and students, but it is the process of learners considering how far they have come that is as valuable as what the teacher will make of that information to inform instruction in the future.

REST

Growing up as a middle-class white woman in the American South, I inherited significant privilege, among them a constant refrain that I "rest," "close my eyes," "put my feet up," and "lie down." My grandmother was a big believer in taking things easy, and she stressed relaxation and quiet as restorative and necessary. While that may have been anachronistic and rooted in outdated gender norms, it inculcated in me a responsibility to myself. I did not realize how rare this emphasis on downtime happened to be until I went to college in New England, where I found the majority of my classmates seemed in constant motion from waking until sleeping and spent any free time engaged in punishing physical activity like distance running or stationary bicycling. Meanwhile, always a morning person, I became a big believer in afternoon naps and bought a television so I could regularly watch the inspirational Oprah Winfrey. I almost always ate off-campus because I appreciated mixing with the life of the town and enjoyed the short walk to get something from a local store, and which was often less expensive than through dining services, too. I read for pleasure, using the local public library as well as the stacks at college. I did well academically, without any significant effort, and I began to learn other strategies about how to build in time for myself. I remember a classmate who would not do any coursework on Saturdays, scheduling that time for herself, and that is a strategy I try to maintain today, with the addition of a cyber-Sabbath. All I could think, watching my classmates spending so much time in knee-jerk motion, was the unsustainable effort they were expending.

If anything, the pace and expectations for industry have only increased in the decades since. The gig economy challenges us to parlay every moment into something concrete and tangible, and late-stage capitalism makes that a necessary reality for too many of us. We see hustle celebrated and time off demonized in the mass media. But without rest, we cannot be creative, or reach the state of flow where we are able to do our best work. This is why I believe the "Pomodoro technique," doing an activity concertedly for 25 minutes and then stopping 5 minutes of recuperation time, can be so valuable. Even if it is a minor percentage of our overall time, we can challenge the pace of modern life and give our bodies and minds time to snap back.

I often see former and current students caught in a state of activity, with so many big picture tasks relegated or forgotten because of the day-to-day demands on their time and attention. A hamster wheel is an apt analogy, but these individuals are merely comical, they are unable to plan for the long term, to say nothing of planning strategically, and they don't have the time to make powerful connections with students and teachers that make the job of school librarian so rewarding. Their responses are knee-jerk rather than considered, and you often get the sense that any small demand might be the straw that breaks the camel's back.

From an administrator's point of view, I would think such activity demonstrates a lack of command and foresight rather than an admirable demonstration of commitment. I still remember my own pride when, teaching a college English course, my department chair came to the door and observed all of the students working concertedly. She was taken aback by their concentration on the task at hand—a sort of exquisite corpse writing activity—and mentioned that most newer instructors felt the need to spend the entire course period in direct instruction. The ability to let the students practice, and to encourage them to do so in directed and specific ways, clearly impressed her. The teacher should not work harder than the student, and modeling calm and reflection is one of the best uses of instructional time.

TIME FOR LEADERSHIP

I think we would all be better off if we devoted twice as much time to half as many commitments. The often-used analogy of radiators and drains is a handy way to analyze our obligations in everything from professional service to community involvement. There are associations that feed us emotionally and spiritually and those that demand time and attention without any visible improvements, the Sisyphean tasks that will never change minds. Our energy, like our time, is finite, and must be budgeted. And, as I asserted in the last chapter, too many school librarians waste time on routine tasks or in trying to complete something they initially postponed. In that vein, too, many school librarians accept committee appointments or volunteer for tasks because we are flattered to be asked without thinking about the real work involved. School librarians need to practice saying "no" to things that will not feed our souls, recognizing that there will be other opportunities to pad our resumes that will offer us real opportunities to grow and do the work we enjoy. One of my friends shared the advice of her department chair, who urged her to weigh each potential commitment with consideration about whether anyone else could do that task.

One of my former teaching colleagues always reminded us with regard to the administration, "They are going to ride the horse they can get the saddle on." Be a little wily and scarce about your participation. Avoid the curse of doing things too well, where competence leads to more responsibilities, harder tasks, and less praise. To be certain, there are many obligations that are a mixed bag—perhaps half of the members of an organization board could take minutes at meetings, but they might be less willing to provide candid counsel for the association president that the role of secretary offers. I would also say that the role of consigliere, of second-in-command, is too often overlooked and underappreciated. As Harry Truman once said, "it is amazing what you can accomplish if you do not care who gets the credit." When you are working with someone whose vision you wholeheartedly support but who can insulate you from criticism, it is an excellent way to change a culture. By focusing on the part of the job that we alone can do and can bring value to, the other aspects become incidental and less of a burden.

The closest I have ever come to professional disagreement evolved from a state library organization Twitter chat I participate in last spring. I tend not to enjoy synchronous chats, but on this particular evening I was online and decided to participate in the conversation. When the discussion turned to leadership, I expressed my own dismay that more librarians did not situate themselves as leaders in the school but instead deferred to teachers and positioned themselves as "less than" the classroom. One of my colleagues voiced that she felt dissuaded from leadership because she did not have the requisite two years' classroom experience to obtain an administrative credential. I tried to explain that the sort of building-based leadership I felt school librarians should aspire to is dispositional rather than positional, and that credentials really weren't a limitation. After all, by the very nature of the school library, the librarian is working in an administrative capacity. I just couldn't understand this sort of refusal to see herself as a leader. Allowing their role to be limited based on a bureaucratic decision on the part of State Department of Education policymakers seemed short-sighted and constricted their instructional reach unnecessarily. This sort of self-limitation seems bound to make you miserable by constraining your professional horizons. My colleague felt that in my poo-pooing the state dictates required for administrative certification, I was endorsing them. Nothing could be further from the truth, but I felt hers was a very narrow definition of leadership.

Perhaps there is something about librarianship that attracts those with respect for the traditional. One of my most difficult tasks as a school library instructor is getting aspiring school librarians to understand there are multiple potential classifications for many nonfiction titles, and that all of these are equally valid. Even as graduate students, new librarians tend to want definitive answers. Understanding ambiguity is the component of realizing your own latitude over organization within the library. I only ask that my students be able to articulate why they have made that choice. Perhaps they have decided that, as a recurring assignment, all of the Lincoln-Douglas debate materials will be collocated into the 940s rather than languishing in rhetoric or the morass that is the social sciences. How can librarians in good conscience leave these materials scattered around the collection?

SLOW READING AND SLOW RESEARCH

Lack of intentionality can be described as compulsive, thoughtless behavior repeated without awareness. Anything done without intentionality can be dangerous. And that includes reading. I know that school librarians devote much of their waking life to beating the drum for independent reading and being the biggest cheerleader in the school for a variety of literacies. But just as there are students who need that encouragement, there are others that will need a "speed bump" to challenge their reading practice. For a handful of students, your challenge might be slowing readers down, moving them from automaticity to a more considered style of reading, or getting them to stop and talk about their reading. Some young people will learn a new appreciation for the works they love if they grapple with writing of their own. Other students may flourish and expand their own reading reach when curating their own recommendations for classmates—sharing the responsibility for reader's advisory is a great way to direct their intellectual energy.

In her 2019 book, *How to Do Nothing: Resisting the Attention Economy*, artist Jenny Odell tracks the tech elite's rejection of digital tools for their own children, coupled with the fact that wealthier individuals have more access to parks and parklands, predicting "gated communities of attention—privileges spaces where some (but not others) can enjoy the fruits of contemplation and the diversification of attention" (Odell 2019, 198–199). This has much application for school libraries. I anticipate there will be more and more ed tech backlash over the next decade as parents and schools realize the limitations of computer systems in instruction. We can provide an alternative, a haven, and a place to make sense of connections outside the virtual.

While the Common Core State Standards promised much in terms of more, smaller research projects integrated across the curriculum, too often this incarnation of research has devolved into retrieval and composition through a single web search. I would advise that anyone interested in helping students grapple with, understand the nature of, and better integrate a range of research embrace the idea of slow research. Have students begin on paper. By not beginning in a browser window, you are already forcing contemplation, and the very act of writing rather than starting at the keyboard forces deliberation. Challenge them to come up with possible search terms, emphasizing synonyms and whole-phrase searching for precision. If you are working within a database, have students turn in the subject terms related to their project before they actually get into the database.

It can be helpful to consider search as a finite resource. I am fortunate enough to have learned retrieval strategies when online research services were still expensive enough that we were encouraged to preplan search strategies. In drafting questions on paper, writing down search terms, mindmapping related concepts to articulate information needs, students will not be able to copy-and-paste from Wikipedia, using its own structure as their own outline. Ask them to contrast their idea of a subject with that they find online or in an encyclopedia. What are the differences in schema? When studying the chemical elements, one student remarked that the author of an article seemed to know exactly what concerns about each item their teacher had sought. That student had not realized that the characteristics of elements would be anticipated and would be common to all matter. You are demonstrating the structure of information as well as how to best connect with it.

At the American Library Association's 2013 Annual Conference, Debbie Abilock and Tasha Bergson Michaelson presented compellingly on adding what they termed "friction" to the student research process. Their focus was in forcing students to articulate their needs and the viability of their findings at each stage in the research process, often asking whether the information is satisfying their information need or merely satisficing it by providing "good enough" information to fulfill the teacher's expectations (Foote 2013). Beginning with her dissertation research, Melissa Gross wrote extensively about "the imposed query," where the student executes a research assignment using the language that the teacher supplies. Gross

(1995) gathered and sorted 369 circulation transactions to inform her theory, which is well regarded within the LIS literature, interviewing each student at the point of checkout to determine whether the transaction was either self-generated or imposed by a teacher, demonstrating that many students did not "own" the question behind the information they sought. The limitations in terms of real understanding linked to such automatic retrieval are obvious.

Paper-based techniques will continue to be useful for those in many fields of life. Virtuoso cartoonist Lynda Barry was asked to come to NASA to talk to scientists about ways of thinking. She said that the phone gives us a lot, but that it also takes away. Barry identified three key elements of discovery—loneliness, uncertainty, and boredom—challenged by being "always on." Barry believed that these elements are where creative ideas came from so she really saw that that mechanism of the delete button, with its ability to quickly remove anything you're unsure of, as eradicating an essential aspect of the necessarily reiterative creative process. By having the ability to erase our work when we find it unsatisfactory, we aren't giving many new ideas a fighting chance. Barry says that writing by hand is "a revelation" for many people today and that there's a different way of thinking that goes along with using one's hands.

JOURNALING TO COMBAT SPEED

You may think of a padded volume with a flimsy lock, but a journal can be a word processing file, an online application, or scribbled in the backs of subject notebooks. In any incarnation, keeping a diary can be a terrific tool for reflection as well as processing feelings and thoughts. Too many would-be diarists get frustrated by the preprinted headings on pages allocated to particular days, something guaranteed to make you feel anxious about staying on task. A blank notebook—I myself prefer those without any lines, or with grids of dots—is an invitation to take oneself and one's existence seriously.

A critical component of mindfulness in school libraries is articulation; this is where journaling can be important. I would advance that we are existing in a moment where forms of journals are being embraced, particularly bullet and list formats, relying on external prompts or layouts copied from online influencers peddling particular lifestyles. But you can easily develop your own subject-specific diaries. These can include the habits one is working on embracing or discarding, music, movies, or reader reflection. If time is truly scarce, it might be helpful to have a monthly reflection or birthday journal. I would suggest that GoodReads and one's Amazon orders and wish list can be viewed as a sort of journal. Anything that dovetails with an individual's passion and interests seems ripe for capturing for posterity or later consideration. "Everyone can find a format and frequency that works for them. It's worth experimenting and trying different methods of journaling until the one that is right for you 'clicks,'" wrote Bill Sannwald (n.d.) on ALA's ODLOS blog.

During the class period allotted for our literary magazine in high school, my teacher encouraged us to journal in a stream-of-consciousness way at the beginning of most class meetings. She was adamant that she would grade them for having been done but that she would not review the content. She urged us to use this as prewriting and brainstorming as well as a release valve for anxieties and pressures of the school day. I still have those journals and treasure them as an artifact of my educational experience. Imagine giving your students the same sort of tangible, long-lasting gift.

I have seen many librarians who include what is perhaps the most common instructional practice of journaling today, that of exit slips, into instruction. I would push that a step and further and consider working with faculty and students around the concept of the commonplace book. The commonplace book developed as a product of eighteenth- and nineteenth-century readers who wanted to save particular passages to commit to memory or for later access. These annotations make for easily accessible talking points when you go to compose an essay, making them an obvious tool. I would advance that students see Instagram and Tumblr as types of journals, albeit ones it is impossible to save offline, keep as private as they might want, and are subject to the vagaries of corporations without concern for privacy or mental well-being.

That is not to say that sharing online is entirely negative. Much social media in the educational community is a form of journaling, documenting practice and sharing ideas, though the value of such sharing has been commodified in our attention economy to the extent where you must curate your feeds ruthlessly to avoid being presented with the same virally popular posts again and again. Try keeping the sharing to yourself. There is an app called 1SE that prompts you to capture one second of video every day. It can be set up to prompt you if you have not recorded by a given time. I can think of few better ways to capture the varied and important roles of school libraries in the lives of students than via video. If you are determined to find an audience, the resulting stitched together experience would make for easy posting to whatever video-based sharing is all the rage at the moment as well as an authentic advocacy tool for sharing with stakeholders.

Young people have begun to reject aspirational incarnations of online sharing. I am hopeful that the newest incarnations of social media are beginning to show a less-polished version of modern life. The aesthetic enabled by filters in Instagram has yielded to a less camera-ready, airbrushed quality, often captured via burst of video instead of static, cropped, manipulated glimpses of amateur product-placement. The rough-and-ready annotation features of SnapChat, designed to be executed in a rush, are at least partially responsible for privileging content over polish. This is a good thing for school libraries.

PROCESS NOT PRODUCT

Research, like journaling, is necessarily a little messy and should be iterative. For too many students, research has become opening a browser window and accepting the top Google search results from whatever query they string together, too often using entirely too many keywords and regurgitating the verbiage of the assignment. Remember that children and young adults often lack the agency to access the resources necessary to fulfill their personal and educational information needs. Virginia Walter (2003) describes young people as fundamentally "information poor," using the small world criteria established by Elfreda Chatman (1991). Walter attributes this information poverty partially to "the low level of communication between adults and children," in addition to the "low status of children in society." Riechel (1991) found children to be systematically disenfranchised in both the school and public library context, with constant reinforcement "that their needs were not as important as those of adults" (p. 6). Though Walter and Riechel were writing before the advent of widespread electronic communications, I think the situation has been exacerbated by myths about the all-knowing digital natives coupled with the post-9/11 desire to shield young people from stressful situations. Gross identified one consequence of information poverty as young people tend to meet their more sensitive information needs "from the media and from other children" (2006, 41).

Artist Jenny Odell, in her 2019 book, *How to Do Nothing*, probes the divergence of technology and nature and the loss of spatial and temporal context afforded by always-connectedness. She calls for readers to "take a protective stance towards ourselves, each other, and whatever is left of what makes us human—including the alliances that sustain and surprise us. I'm suggesting we protect our *spaces* and our *time* for non-instrumental, non-commercial activity and thought, for maintenance, for art, for conviviality" (p. 28). By slowing down and focusing on the individual and how you can help them, you are providing not only a home away from home, but a school away from school. And it is up to school librarians to always return to students' needs.

REFERENCES

Chatman, Elfreda A. 1991. "Life in a Small World: Applicability of Gratification Theory to Information-Seeking Behavior." *Journal of American Society for Information Science* 42, no. 6: 438–449.

Foote, Carolyn. 2013. "Slow Thinking and Research—Bridging the Gap." *Futura*. July 25, 2013. https://futura.edublogs.org/2013/07/25/slow-thinking-and-research-bridging-the-gap/.

Gross, Melissa. 1995. "The Imposed Query." *Reference Quarterly* 35, no. 2: 236–243.

Gross, Melissa. 2006. *Studying Children's Questions: Imposed and Self-generated Information Seeking at School*. Lanham, MD: Scarecrow.

Odell, Jenny. 2019. *How to Do Nothing: Resisting the Attention Economy*. Brooklyn, NY: Melville House.

Riechel, Rosemarie. 1991. *Reference Services for Children and Young Adults*. Hamden, CT: Show String Press.

Sannwald, Bill. n.d. "Self-Care for Librarians: Journaling." Intersections. http://www.ala.org/advocacy/diversity/odlos-blog/self-care-journaling.

Walter, Virginia A. 2003. "Public Library Service to Children and Teens: A Research Agenda." *Library Trends* 51, no. 4: 571–589.

SIX

Whole-School Advocacy for Students

When I enrolled in education coursework more than two decades ago, the presumption was that students came to school ready to learn and with the necessary supports in place at home. No one talked about students that might be hungry, tired, living in less-than-ideal circumstances or homeless. Any suggestion that these children might not be teachable was seen to be abandoning the chief role of education in imparting knowledge and, indeed, civilization for future generations. Similarly, when we look at literature around educational efficacy and statistically significant attainment, oftentimes instruction appears to have occurred in a vacuum. But we all know that not every child comes to school every day prepared psychologically or physically to engage with content, their peers, or their teachers.

While it has long been accepted that schools are in loco parentis for student physical well-being, student emotional health and its role in education are less explored. Schools, suffering from an increasing sense of mission creep, may resist taking another dimension of student life under its auspices. And, as teachers, we can be hesitant to intervene when we have the sense that conflict or misunderstanding is culturally rooted. Nonetheless, teaching SEL in heterogenous classes and schools are both more difficult and more necessary, and part of a necessary "ethics of care."

Social and emotional needs can be difficult to assess and address in a busy classroom or library environment as they are needs that might not be expressed by learners through behavior or words. Nonetheless, schoolwide policies and practices can contribute to student security and growth for all learners. The space needs to contain predictable and safe environments with attention to transitions and sensory needs. Teachers need to learn about and constantly consider the role that trauma and other elements of children's home lives may be playing in learning difficulties. Administrators should provide collaborative opportunities for confidential conversations about students and involve the whole faculty in safety planning including limiting access to personal student information and enforcement of legal and court orders. While "emotional practice is still catching up to the emotional science," wrote Heller (2017), "more and more people are coming to recognize that unless kids feel emotionally safe and unless they have the skills and language they need to manage their emotions, they will struggle in and out of school" (p. 24).

Classroom strategies can also be structured in ways that will serve students well, but especially those who need extra support. Expectations can be communicated positively rather than punitively, individual interests should be validated and encouraged, and students should have opportunities to practice regulating emotion and moderating behavior. We can learn much from the school and teachers who have embraced this student-centered work.

DEFINING SOCIAL-EMOTIONAL LEARNING

Social-emotional learning (SEL) "is a deceptively simple label attached to an enormously complex range of issues" (Gehlbach 2017, 9). Most generally, SEL can be seen as a method of promoting holistic child development by teaching students skills like self-regulation, persistence, empathy, self-awareness, and mindfulness. But at the root of SEL lies in improving relationships and the communications that inform those. At the core of SEL "lies a single, teachable capacity that anchors almost all of our social interactions: Social perspective taking, or the capacity to make sense of others' thoughts and feelings" (Gehlbach 2017, 10). Gehlbach equates this to "adopting the mindset of a detective rather than a judge" (11).

SEL can be positioned as an outgrowth of efforts to improve climate and overall achievement. "A majority of teachers and principals are measuring school climate—whether students feel safe to learn, whether they have good relationships with adults—but fewer are testing how well students can demonstrate actual social-emotional skills like self-management, compassion and taking someone else's perspective" (Stringer 2019). At Langley Elementary in the Washington, D.C., public schools, each student is greeted in the morning by administrators to gauge how students are feeling at the beginning of the day and intervene as necessary. There is an emphasis on an appropriate transition to the school space, setting students up to get rid of any stresses, both in the morning and throughout the day to relieve tension and anxiety. D.C.'s Dean of Students Monique Robinson says there are four main components that make up daily SEL sessions there: an activity to unite, an activity to disengage, an activity to connect and an activity to commit. These activities will look different depending on the student population and the general climate, but allowing for reaction to the news of the day, marking the rhythms of the calendar and the school year, and providing creative outlets that extend learning in tangible ways are all aspects of SEL. The celebrations of the 100th day or school or Pi Day arts and crafts are ways to integrate SEL in ways that also address curricular objectives. I remember one colleague who allowed her practical math students to illustrate concepts like ratios and proportions for extra credit. She accepted and displayed only the best student work in her classroom, and her students became quite competitive about the products and even become more interested in data visualization in the abstract.

Advisory periods have become common ways for faculty to have non-curricular interactions with students, often structuring that through a "home base" where students are grouped within or across grades without consideration of ability. Administrators who add advisory time to the master schedule base that decision upon considerations that developing stronger teacher-student relationships will improve student achievement. In practice, some schools might use the time for study hall, and others used it for announcements or character development. But structured protocols and conferencing around academic progress and goals "empowers students to take ownership of their grades and learning and see their growth over time" (Bailey 2018).

There are many existing curriculums related to promoting SEL, so no one needs to reinvent the wheel. Among them is a 12-week mindfulness-based Kindness Curriculum emphasizing executive function, self-regulation, and prosocial behavior, and MindUP, a mindfulness and meditation curriculum promoted by Goldie Hawn's foundation. Another programmatic approach to SEL, the RULER suite of training and online tools available through Yale's Center for Emotional Intelligence, uses a gradated Mood Meter with axes labeled energy and feeling. Students are coached to track their position among the hundred labeled squares, using RULER's "feelings words" to establish a common, school-wide vocabulary.

To ensure the success of SEL, a RAND report found several necessary conditions:

1. It is important to demonstrate to educators that SEL can lead to benefits and that it can support, rather than detract from, work to improve student academic achievement.
2. SEL supports should build students' social and emotional strengths and not simply address behavioral challenges.
3. Those who support educators to implement SEL programs and curricula should consider ways to help teachers and school leaders integrate SEL into content area instruction. (Hamilton, Doss, and Steiner 2019)

There is a growing body of research to support SEL as it relates to achievement.

The Collaborative for Academic, Social and Emotional Learning (CASEL 2019) finds students who participate in evidence-based SEL programs showed "an 11 percent gain in academic achievement. They stay in school longer, make healthier life choices and are more likely to be civically engaged." A 2011 meta-analysis of more than 200 SEL programs found that students receiving explicit SEL curricula performed 11 percentage points better in academic achievement and demonstrated superior emotional skills and attitudes than their peers who didn't participate, and a 2016 study of 82 programs found that "even after 3½ years, the benefits of social-emotional learning programs persisted, as participating students scored 13 points higher in academics, and had 6 percent higher graduation rates, and 11 percent better college attendance rates" (Stringer 2019).

HOW CAN SEL HELP DISADVANTAGED STUDENTS?

Learning to regulate emotions is an important part of childhood development, but it is especially critical for students who come from stressful backgrounds. Oftentimes, factors like violence, abuse, neglect, and hunger have shaped our students' development and made them reactive rather than proactive. Oftentimes, slowing down the response to stimuli is critical. RULER features a technique called the meta-moment "stepping back and considering how to respond through the lens of your 'best self'" (Heller 2017, 22–23). Learning to acknowledge and manage responses through steps like deep breathing, taking time out, and practicing mindfulness have proven effective for improving the climate among students and teachers.

Hayden Frederick-Clarke, director of cultural proficiency at the Boston Public Schools, likewise stressed that schools need to be careful about imposing the cultural norms of white teachers onto students from other backgrounds. Otherwise, he said, social and emotional learning can turn into "acculturation and assimilation activities" (Diallo 2019). "Putting teachers in charge of deciding which students are socially competent raises concerns that educators' unconscious biases could creep into the evaluation process, disproportionately penalizing students of color." At the DC school where SEL has proven effective, Robinson (2019) stresses that the school's teachers have been trained in the importance of culturally responsive teaching, especially race and implicit bias and that teachers have been hired based in part on their understanding of, and commitment to, the school's approach to social and emotional learning. Nonetheless, "there are critics who contend that instilling social values in students is the purview of parents not schools, and others who fear that SEL could easily be used as yet another way to punish low-income students of color who don't conform to behavioral norms" (Diallo 2019). Any SEL implementation needs to take care to be culturally sensitive and avoid imposing narrow behaviors.

SKILLS AND STRATEGIES

Key social-emotional skills can be infused into more traditional academic work, Darling-Hammond reinforces, pointing to skills like perseverance and resilience when learning to revise an essay, or group work that teaches interpersonal skills (Ferlazzo 2019). Constructivist group work is one instructional strategy that involves students working together to learn how to interact effectively and constructively, and a project that ends in a class presentation involves a student's communication skills. In Washington, D.C., Capital City educators said they take steps to ensure that their process is fair and geared toward helping students improve. Students are measured on traits like reflection and accountability in the context of their academic work. "A research-heavy science project that involves numerous revisions and multiple draft deadlines, for example, provides an opportunity for a student to demonstrate organization and punctuality skills" (Robinson 2019).

Sharing coping skills can be inclusive and make conscious existing strategies to minimize stress or conflict in a positive and constructive way. Students can compile a list of their own preferred strategies, and the class can collaborate to make an inventory listing various techniques that can be duplicated or posted as reminder of potential reactions to stressors. Metacognition is central. Some schools, especially elementary ones, may provide a quick inventory for students to stop and refocus, including "tapping," a routine that focuses the attention on certain pulse points in an effort to reorient consciousness to focus or when experiencing conflict or upset in the classroom (read more on tapping in chapter 7). A version of this for older students might be based on Jace Harr's (n.d.) popular online interactive, effectively walking an upset individual through an inventory related to mood, medication, sleep, pain, temperature regulation, and even making sure that students are engaging in critical self-care like showering.

To strengthen practical application and maintenance of coping skills, teacher Michele Lew builds time into each class period for an exercise she calls the "5 Minute Fix." "For five minutes, students can share how they've used their coping skills in real-life situations. They can ask for feedback and advice from peers or provide suggestions to those who are struggling. Most importantly, the community is strengthened by these daily check-ins. Allocating five minutes doesn't interfere with my academic lessons, and the benefit to students is significant and impactful" (Lew 2018). These strategies will benefit every student. In fact, "those who were the best in the class found it much harder to persist when faced with challenges" (Stringer 2019).

Teacher Amanda Wandishion's fourth-grade class at Elizabeth Shelton School in Wandishion, Connecticut, uses SEL to help students learn to hone their speaking abilities and build confidence. She established "Feel Good Friday," a weekly exercise, where students praise their classmates via a written note. The lesson teaches them the importance of empathy in society, Wandishion said. "More and more colleges and workplaces are recognizing that soft skills are valuable," said Wandishion. "This type of learning provides a foundation for them to be successful, now and in the future" (Sample 2019).

At Capital City in northwest D.C., social and emotional learning is woven into daily interactions between adults and students and integrated into classroom content. "Many students are quick to link outcomes like good grades to personal characteristics of persistence, self-confidence and the ability to manage their time wisely" (Robinson 2019). Many of these traits can be considered those necessary for leaders, something many schools aspire to produce. Most successful people are self-aware, effective communicators, problem solvers, collaborative and can persevere in the face of obstacles and adversity. Schools are also uniquely positioned to support resilience in brains still benefiting from the neuroplasticity of youth, and in many cases can inform successful coping against adverse outcomes after exposure to traumatic experiences.

Many school librarians will remember reference services lessons cautioning against providing medical or legal advice in particular. I would argue that wellness is a different mindset and one that can involve whole-school efforts informed by "ethics of care," a concept that sociologist Nel Noddings evolved that is considered to be a form of relational ethics because it prioritizes concern for relationships between individuals.

Unlike legal areas, every school has specialized staff devoted to health and physical instruction. School nurses are often eager to become involved in broader education efforts, as are physical education and health teachers. Not enough teachers use the whole-school staff, but it is necessary to build an inclusive team and communicate student needs across departments. This will reap additional benefits in developing the collaborative culture all librarians seek.

REFERENCES

Bailey, James. 2018. "Making Advisory More Effective." *Edutopia.* November 1, 2018. https://www.cdutopia.org/article/making-advisory-more-effective.

Collaborative for Academic, Social and Emotional Learning (CASEL). 2019. "Impact." https://casel.org/impact/.

Diallo, Amadou. 2019. "A School Where Character Matters as Much as Academics." *Hechinger Report.* September 3, 2019. https://hechingerreport.org/a-school-where-character-matters-as-much-as-academics/.

Ferlazzo, Larry. 2019. "Classroom Q&A: A 'Trauma-Informed Classroom Is a Safe and Secure Place.'" *Education Week.* May 21, 2019. http://blogs.edweek.org/teachers/classroom_qa_with_larry_ferlazzo

/2019/05/response_a_trauma_informed_classroom_is_a_safe
_and_secure_place.html.

Gehlbach, Hunter. 2017. "Learning to Walk in Another's Shoes." *Phi Delta Kappan* 98, no. 6 (March): 8–12.

Hamilton, Laura S., Christopher Joseph Doss, and Elizabeth D. Steiner. 2019. "Teacher and Principal Perspectives on Social and Emotional Learning in America's Schools: Findings from the American Educator Panels." RAND. https://www.rand.org/pubs/research_reports /RR2991.html.

Harr, Jace. (n.d.) "Self-Care Interactive." http://philome.la/jace_harr /you-feel-like-shit-an-interactive-self-care-guide/play.

Heller, Rafael. 2017. "On the Science and Teaching of Emotional Intelligence: An Interview with Marc Brackett." *Phi Delta Kappan* 98, no. 6 (March): 20–24.

Lew, Michele. 2018. "A 4-Step Process for Building Student Resilience." *Edutopia.* November 7, 2018. https://www.edutopia.org/article/ 4-step-process-building-student-resilience.

Robinson, Monique. 2019. "How SEL Transformed Our School." *SmartBrief.* July 16, 2019. https://www.smartbrief.com/original/2019/07 /how-sel-transformed-our-school.

Sample, Robert. 2019. "A Shelton Fourth-Grade Teacher Puts the Kids in Charge." *CT Post.* January 21, 2019. https://www.ctpost.com/local /article/A-Shelton-fourth-grade-teacher-puts-the-kids-in-13550206 .php.

Stringer, Kate. 2019. "Most Educators Assess Their Students' Social-Emotional Learning, but Few See the Whole Picture. Here's What They're Missing." *The 74 Million.* July 10, 2019. https://www .the74million.org/article/most-educators-assess-their-students -social-emotional-learning-but-few-see-the-whole-picture-heres -what-theyre-missing.

SEVEN

Physical Fitness and Well-Being

MENS SANS IN CORPORE SANO

This section takes its title from the Latin phrase, translated as "a healthy mind in a healthy body," used to express the theory that physical exercise is an important or essential part of overall health. This is a lofty goal for any school and one that does not require funding or equipment when directed motion is a part of the school experience.

In 2018, a viral video captured at Ninian's Primary School in Stirling depicted uniformed Scottish youngsters gleefully running around their red brick building in an activity they have dubbed the Daily Mile. For five years, this school has devoted a scant amount of time, 15 minutes, to get students fully awake by running around the building each morning, getting outside in an active and communal way. As captured, this seems a blissful experience for all concerned. Consider how many disciplinary issues this simple, whole-school activity eliminates. And it has been proven effective. Research findings show that the Daily Mile intervention is effective at increasing levels of moderate to vigorous intensity physical activity, reducing sedentary time, increasing physical fitness and improving body composition (Chesham et al. 2018). The Daily Mile study includes an interesting shorthand acronym for the concerns of the study: WHEEL, or Well-being, Health, Exercise, Enjoyment and Learning. Those elements reflect the holistic effects of physical activity rather than focusing narrowly on strength and aerobic fitness.

The whole topic of human bodies and wellness is so fraught and laden that it can be difficult to have a conversation about it. Most of our working conditions are ergonomic nightmares, with carpal tunnel par for the course for too many librarians. But we live in our bodies, and we only have one. Think of when you carry something heavy, say a ream of paper, upstairs. You cannot disavow the strain excess weight places on you. While, yes, media images of women in particular are unnecessarily restrictive in ideals of fitness and beauty, and you can be healthy at any size, it is important to realize our body's limitations and work within those to be the best we can be.

Every workplace I have had has the co-workers who, given any lull in conversation, resort to diet or weight loss as a topic. This does no one any good. As one assistant principal told me, those who talk about it are least likely to do something about it. Nonetheless, we all know that there are foods which are better for our bodies. Some of us have sensitivities to particular ingredients, but processed foods are no good for anyone, even if they are less expensive and handier. We all get too much sugar, and we all can use a walk around the block. Often the best remedy for physical ills is providing alternatives—not just packages cookies, but apples, having a cheese pizza as well as pepperoni, taking the field trip to Subway, where there are a range of options, instead of McDonalds. This is important to remember for in-school library programs, where I see a dependence on junk food and cheap sugar as incentive to bring students in the door. We need to honor our students' bodies by feeding them well.

ACTIVITY, NOT EXERCISE

Any librarian who has used a wearable fitness tracker has probably noticed that they easily get their recommended "steps" in through the day in a busy library. But contrast that with your students' activity levels. It is easy to become immobile, especially when engrossed at computer stations or looking at handheld devices where they can easily lose track of time. We all have seen headlines about the mortality of those with sedentary lives. This is why the Pomodoro technique is so powerful, in urging you to shift states, which often means physical positions, regularly. The Pomodoro signal to periodically change activities stresses increased productivity, but that shift can make you more active without even realizing it.

While it would be wonderful if everyone could experience the endorphins from long-distance running or triathlon training, this sort of aerobic activity will never be for everyone. Doubtless there are many library-goers who often experience exercise as sweaty, smelly, and punishing, to say nothing of the interpersonal aggression that can manifest in gyms and on sports fields. Compound this with the vulnerability of older students in many physical education programs, where they can be made to strip to change clothes to "dress out," and you can understand student reluctance to participate in anything reminiscent of physical education. For Langley Elementary in the D.C. public schools, part of social emotional learning involves ensuring that recess is a positive, safe, and meaningful time and space. "If recess is often not as safe as it could be, it can promote division among students" (Robinson 2019). Since physical education coursework is often legally mandated, the vulnerability of many students in these settings is considerable. But there are ways to promote gentle activity without shaming students who might not be moving around enough.

Too many people conflate exercise and activity. Even modest activity like walking leads to better sleep, focus, and acuity for us and our students. There are small adjustments we can make in our space to promote wellness. Varying décor can help. Standing desks for OPACs, and search and printing stations are one option for allowing the fidgety (or the very tall) access without the constraint of being seated. Tall and very low tables provide some built-in stretching and an opportunity to swing their legs to expel nervous energy, and beanbags, balance ball and molded foam seating can also allow for a wider range of physical positions than traditional chairs. Handheld weights, balance boards, a Wii Fit, and jump ropes are all easy to add to library spaces (and things you can probably get donated from those who bought the kit but failed to live up to New Year's resolutions).

One easy way to get more activity happening in your space is using the dimensions of the library itself as a teachable moment. When studying geography, assign students a state or country and then have them position themselves to create a three-dimensional representation of relative locations. The same strategy can be used linearly. If students are researching the elements, they can sort themselves in a line based on the atomic weight. This makes the learning sticky, especially for kinesthetic learners who can see relationships between objects better when they are manifest physically. You can use this same sorting strategy to work on directional awareness or mood. I asked my advisory students to sort themselves into lines and corners based on how they responded to particular affective prompts.

You can also use representation of distance to build data literacy as well as physical activity. When the cooperative summer reading theme focused on wellness, Matt Layne at the Emmett O'Neal Library in Mountain Brook, Alabama, used Tolkein's geography to gamify physical activity.

Teens could participate in "a walk from the Shire," with Mordor a distant 1,779 miles away. Using a poster as leaderboard, young people could track their relative progress against their peers over time towards that destination. Physical activity can also be incorporated into the school library space by using stationary bikes. This received great attention at The Falls Church High School library in Virginia, where Carrie Kausch works, which installed four stationary bicycles, situated to look outdoors, so that students could pedal while they read. As any early childhood educator will tell you, one of the advantages to using learning stations is the built-in motion from one area to the next.

PLAY

In younger children, aerobic exercise is often the result of free play. But, with concerns about vulnerability outdoors and an increase in screentime for youngsters, children are playing far less than in previous generations. Consultant Anna Beam believes that "children have become less emotionally expressive, less talkative, and less imaginative over the past two decades. One prescription for this illness is social-emotional play. By encouraging conversation, playing games, and setting aside time for open social play, children can develop these critical skills needed to be good students and citizens" (Beam 2018). This is a tragic loss, as young mammals of every species play, an activity that not only teaches them how to interact with their peers but has been demonstrated to reduce fear, anxiety, stress, and irritability. Play within the school day offers students the opportunity to shift into a receptive and imaginative state, and regulated play often shuts down any "risk play" where youngsters can "experience fear without losing their heads" (Beam 2018).

One of the best things we can do for students and ourselves is modeling a range of healthy lifestyles. When I think about the older people I know who practice even mild exercises like Jazzercise or water aerobics, they have better posture and more flexibility and strength than more sedentary cohorts. I worked with a veteran teacher who would walk the track, often circling around the physical education students, during her planning period. She was also very vocal about fasting one day a week, citing scripture that presented fasting as a spiritual obligation. She also retired the moment she was able, demonstrating an enviable work-life balance. I learned much from being around her.

If you feel unable to build in the time commitment required for regular exercise, determine to seize opportunities to be active in bursts. There are many physical undertakings that can be accomplished in smaller segments. If you are trying to get more active, try blocking concentrated activity into 20 minute spans. Be it washing the car, weeding or other gardening, scrubbing the bathtub or even shopping for vegetables or kneading bread, focusing on these tasks can increase your physicality in the moment. Anything that raises your heart rate is going to be beneficial. Perhaps during the work week, you can aim for 20 minutes each day, while aiming for three 20 minute segments of varying activity over the weekends. And the more active you are, the less neighborhood walks, leisurely bike rides, and yoga outdoors will feel like exercise.

MEDITATION OR FOCUS

While a state of focused "flow" might be optimal for many creative and constructive enterprises, too often students are left alone to passively consume media (think of the rise of "binge" as associated with "watching"). School issued iPads always seem to me to be more about consumption than creation and remind me of Aldous Huxley's prescient description of a sedating substance that inures the user to life; *soma is* the "ideal pleasure drug" in his novel *Brave New World* (1932), and while its chemistry and pharmacology are undefined, as described, the drug resembles a tranquilizer or an opiate. The iPads, a parent and substitute teacher observed, keep the students quiet and docile. Increasingly, I think we as a culture have begun to challenge whether that is desirable in a citizenry.

In contrast to *soma*, mindfulness meditation emphasizes noticing, observing, and fully experiencing bodily sensations and works on stilling the mind. Studying meditation, we are constantly reminded to let thoughts come into our minds, to acknowledge and accept them, but ultimately to let them leave us. Many experienced meditators can tune out distractions to achieve a more receptive state where the mind remains open and still.

In our always-on, connected culture, focus can be difficult to achieve. Despite recent lip-service on the part of big technology companies to concerns around work-life balance, time management, and the installation of applications to tell you just what you are spending your time doing, mobile devices are designed to reinforce their constant use. The pings of notifications give us a sense of belonging, of connection. But the perpetual monitoring of electronics takes a toll on the body as well as the psyche. Look around you in any crowd and I would wager you see the ill effects of mobile devices on posture. Think of the skeletons that were altered almost beyond recognition by whalebone corsets. Constant handheld viewing and input are physically altering young people, even if we are not sure of the end effects upon physiognomy (Apkan 2019).

YOGA OR STRETCHING

In popular culture, yoga has been hijacked by Lulemon-wearing refugees from aerobics class, performing flows at breakneck pace. When I first took yoga in college, my instructor was an enormous woman named Jyoti who was a devotee of the Iyengar school of micromovement. We met for 90 minutes, three times a week, and it seemed we spent a very long time in savasana and doing mat exercises. It was some of the hardest physical and psychological work I have ever done. For someone who came from a family that was not physically demonstrative, having a relative stranger touch me nonjudgmentally to correct my form was also emotionally charged. But I can honestly say that after a semester with Jyoti, it seemed like I was never NOT doing yoga.

Today, an estimated 8.7 percent of the U.S. population practice some form of yoga.

There are number of librarians at various levels who have worked on sharing yoga with students as a way to focus and provide gentle physical activity. In 2015, *School Library Journal* profiled elementary librarian Tracy Wong at PS 54 Fordham Bedford Academy in the Bronx, who sits on the floor alongside her students to guide them through poses on the floor in the school library space. "Yoga gives them the resources to calmly react to stressful situations—at school or anywhere. She doesn't obtain release forms from parents, nor does she involve the administration. To Wong, yoga is less a workout than a way for her students to find calm" (Barack 2015).

There seems a natural affinity between people attracted to libraries and yoga. Both are traditionally quiet and reflective. I have heard concerns from librarians that hosting yoga is usurping the role of physical educators or community centers. But there are individuals who will attend physical activities in a library space that would never attend the same event in an exercise studio. When planning to bring yoga into your space, look for practitioners and sessions labeled as gentle to ensure that the program will be accessible to the widest variety of participants. If you are sharing videos, you can showcase a range of nontraditional yogis and yoginis including Ally McGraw, Rodney Yee, and Jessamyn Stanley. You can research chair and desk yoga, and seek the support of practitioners who have a curriculum honed working with those with physical limitations in nursing homes. In my own state of Alabama, the established Four-H program has yoga instructors in every county. I have been to several of their sessions, which feature gentle moves that emphasize the need to stretch in six directions.

Many schools that have attempted to implement mindfulness have faced criticism, either for indoctrinating young people in Eastern religion, or in supporting spiritual practices that violate separation of church and state. Two legal cases often cited when considering whether spiritual content can be taught are *Lemon v. Kurtzman* (1971), which dealt with public funding streams for parochial schools and *Edwards v. Aguillard* (1987), concerning the constitutionality of teaching creationism. In my own state, Alabama, yoga is explicitly prohibited under state code due to its religious roots in Hinduism. ALSDE said teachers may instruct students on poses, exercises and stretches associated with the practice as long as the course is not called yoga. Forms of meditation—those that focusing on a mantra, or repeated word or phrase—are also banned. Because of the potential spiritual associations, the Four-H was very clear that they never use Sanskrit words with their public groups. Tai'chi, which has been used in the United Kingdom to reduce stress associated with high pressure examinations (Turner 2019), is not explicitly prohibited. Your state might still ban yoga and meditation as practices, but it is more difficult to excise secular stretching and breathing.

BREATHWORK

No-cost, do-anywhere communal breathwork is perhaps one of the easiest-to-implement strategies for increasing mindfulness and focus in any space or among any student group. Janet Bavonese calls breathing "a remote control for the nervous system (2019)." Dr. Andrew Weil (2014) claims that breathwork, using a 4-7-8 count to represent the inhale through the nose, holding the breath with the diaphragm, and expelling through the mouth, can be as effective as prescription tranquilizers.

When working with younger students, you may use phrases like box breathing or balloon breathing emphasizing working from the diaphragm. Repeated deep breathing oxygenates the blood and enables a shift in physiology. Ashley Neese (2019) authored an excellent primer on breathwork, situating the practice as a necessary coping mechanism. "The experience of being overwhelmed by thoughts and emotions is often a marker of trauma. Trauma is anything that we experience as a threat to our survival or overall well-being. These threats register in our nervous system, and if the natural restoration process is interrupted, coping mechanisms are put in place to survive the experiences. If left unprocessed, these coping mechanisms may lead to belief and behavioral changes that create patterns that are difficult to heal without addressing, the body, the nervous system, and the breath" (Neese 2019). Among the 25 exercises she highlights, Neese describes a series of energy breaths with arms held high to both inspire or diffuse energy, a focus breath with vocalization, and a joy breath that involves holding your breath briefly before laughing. Most of her exercises take around five minutes, which makes them perfect for transitions in school settings.

SENSORY FOCUS

Even disconnected from audio, over-the-ear headphones are an easy way to allow students the option to tune out when things get overwhelming. It seems like more and more public spaces are realizing that students with sensory issues can benefit from these noise cancelling effects, and more families travel with their own. Think about the policies in your school regarding electronics. Do they make a provision for students who might need these to adjust to the noise volume in their classroom or in public spaces in between classes?

Public libraries' youth services staff are really inspirational on many levels, but especially so when it comes to how they have embraced the sensory storytime movement. Sensory storytimes are often structured around interactive small group work with preschoolers, especially those with special needs. For students who need support, part of planning can involve creating microenvironments that are themselves comforting and inclusive. This can be of particular benefit for young people on the autism spectrum or other sensory processing issues. The sensation of being enclosed is one that many students find to be supportive and protective.

Sturdy carboard boxes can be repurposed to create individual seats—add paper plate wheels and you can have an ersatz racecar—rather than having students sit on the floor or with their limbs out. Plastic storage tubs can be easily modified by cutting half the lid to produce a contained "bucket seat." Tubs have the advantage of being easily stackable for storage.

You can also create this sort of isolated, concentrated space via reading tents, which are a huge trend in elementary school classrooms as well as libraries. I have seen old clawfoot bathtubs repurposed as special reading stations, replete with pillows where students had the opportunity to curl up with a book. The whole idea of idea of getting comfortable with a book, putting your feet up at or above your heart, or curling up on a couch signals ownership of the space and allows creating assertive home-like or nest-like environments.

If we are successful in making students comfortable, that it seems a natural outgrowth that students would want to be in a library space especially when they are exhausted can't concentrate or didn't feel well. You can tell a lot about libraries, especially high school libraries, by how they respond to students who are napping in the space. Are you seeing this as a pressing physical need to be respected before the student returns to instruction? Consider the many workplaces who have adopted this trend on corporate campuses.

Believe it or not, there are many library spaces that have created dedicated sleeping space, either through nap pods or nap rooms, for students. Purpose-built nap pods are essentially recliners with a way to effectively seclude your sightline from the rest of the environment, sort of like a first-class capsule on an airline. One study of the efficacy of nap pods centered on students in a university library setting. Those reported feeling agitated or upset were assigned to spend 20 minutes in a pod. A 20-minute "disco nap" is enough to recharge without getting into the deeper stages of sleep. Students who used the pods reported that they all felt more rested happier and more in control of their emotions. Access to the sleep when they need it supports student self-regulation.

At New Milford High School in New Jersey, librarian Laura Fleming created a nap room adjacent to the library. To ensure supervision, the door had been taken off the hinges but the lights were dimmed and there were several recliners where students who'd needed to take a break during the day can come in and do just that. Allowing for students to recharge recognizes and respects the complexities of their lives. By creating a dedicated space, be it for quiet, sleep, or physical activity, you are helping to normalize physical regulation and create a caring environment that really focuses on student needs.

PHYSICAL REGULATION

One slightly "out there" physical learning strategy that had gained influence in school communities is that of "tapping." My colleague Professor Valerie Wheat became interested in tapping when she saw TeacherTube videos, where tapping was part of school or class culture, using that physical activity as an aid to self-regulation and soothing (2019, also mentioned in chapter 6). The tapping process involves sequentially touching pressure points on your face and chest; Wheat asserts that this process can resituate the student in the here and now and can be used for conflict resolution, especially among students with learning differences ("The Tapping Solution," 2020). Tapping as a strategy is rooted in the Emotional Freedom Technique (EFT) and also emphasizes deep breathing. For those interested in introducing this to students, Wheat recommends two related apps, Tap Around the Clock and The Tapping Solution, which also has a well-developed website with videos, diagrams, and research findings related to EFT and tapping: https://www.thetappingsolution.com/what-is-eft-tapping/. Is tapping more effective than asking students to count to ten or even just to take a deep breath? Perhaps the valuable component is establishing and acknowledging the pressure of our bodies under stress and sharing strategies for managing it.

REFERENCES

Apkan, Nsikan. 2019. "Smartphones Aren't Making Millennials Grow Horns. Here's How to Spot a Bad Study." PBS Newshour. June 25, 2019. https://www.pbs.org/newshour/science/smartphones-arent -making-millennials-grow-horns-heres-how-to-spot-a-bad-study.

Barack, Lauren. 2015. "Yoga in the Library." *School Library Journal*. January 15, 2015. http://www.slj.com/?detailStory=yoga-in-the-library.

Bavonese, Janet. 2019. "Classroom Calm Down." CORE Academy Presentation. June 4, 2019. Jacksonville State University.

Beam, Natalie D. 2018. "Crisis in Play." Louisiana Library Association Annual Convention Presentation. March 8, 2018. Alexandria, LA.

Chesham, Ross A., Josephine N. Booth, Emma L. Sweeney, Gemma C. Ryde, Trish Gorely, Naomi E. Broks, and Colin N. Moran. 2018. "The Daily Mile Makes Primary School Children More Active, Less Sedentary and Improves Their Fitness and Body Composition: A Quasi-Experimental Pilot Study." May 20, 2018. https://bmcmedicine.biomedcentral.com/articles/10.1186/s12916-018-1049-z.

Huxley, Aldous. 1932. *Brave New World.* http://uploads.worldlibrary.org/uploads/pdf/201706222311052015_463582_brave_new_world.pdf.

Neese, Ashley. 2019. *How to Breathe: 25 Simple Practices for Calm, Joy and Resilience.* Berkeley, CA: Ten Speed Press.

Robinson, Monique. 2019. "How SEL Transformed Our School." *SmartBrief.* July 16, 2019. https://www.smartbrief.com/original/2019/07/how-sel-transformed-our-school.

"The Tapping Solution." 2020. "What Is Tapping?" https://www.thetappingsolution.com/what-is-eft-tapping/.

Turner, Camilla. 2019. "T'ai Chi Is Being Taught in Primary Schools to Help Children Overcome Exam Stress." The Telegraph. June 1, 2019. https://www.telegraph.co.uk/education/2019/06/01/tai-chi-taught-primary-schools-help-children-overcome-exam-stress/.

Weil, Andrew. 2014. "4-7-8 Breathing." https://www.drweil.com/videos-features/videos/breathing-exercises-4-7-8-breath/.

Wheat, Valerie. 2019. "Tap Away the Stress." CORE Academy Presentation. June 4, 2019. Jacksonville State University.

EIGHT

Safety and Other Student Needs

As a part of accreditation preparation, students are sometimes given inventories that include questions asking how they feel about different aspects of their school experiences. In both institutions where I worked, the administration regularly shook their heads about results revealing that a sizeable number of students never felt safe in school. While schools invest in training to spot and mitigate bullying behavior, including the sorts of SEL efforts discussed in chapter 6, an asocial environment can be more difficult to pinpoint or treat.

THE WORK OF LYNNE EVARTS

I was very fortunate that, soon after becoming a school librarian, I was exposed to the inspirational work of Lynne Evarts, a Wisconsin high school media specialist who presented at the first American Association of School Librarians (AASL) national conference that I attended in Pittsburgh in 2005. Her concern with prioritizing authentic, trusting relationships with students and integrating knowledge of their cultures, interests, concerns, fears, and triggers situates her among the godmothers of the field of mindful librarianship in school settings. In that AASL session, she described her school library as "a sanctuary," and she shared many stories about how students who didn't have a lot of support either within the school or at home found necessary advocacy and community in the library. I knew I had found a model for how I wanted my space to support students, and I would seek out Evarts's presentations at subsequent AASL conferences.

Evarts was candid in admitting that oftentimes the students who found their way to her space had a lot of social and emotional issues and were marginalized among their peers. Oftentimes, they openly shared that they had a lot of things going on at home and lacked a caring adult to talk to. She talked a lot about the bibliotherapeutic aspect of reading, about how literature about people who were both like you and different from you could provide integral information, and how books could be tremendous comfort, as any avid reader knows. Evarts captured the essence of her philosophy in a 2006 article for VOYA, which looks at what she terms "isolated students," a category she says she herself fell into in school, and how the library can provide connection and safety. "Librarians have a head start because isolated teens are already hanging out in the library. All we need to do is reach out to them."

In her Voice of Youth Advocates (VOYA) piece, Evarts evokes the Columbine shootings: "Unfortunately that culture of isolation and feeling of not being safe continues to pervade high schools almost eight years later. Fortunately, there is a way that school librarians can wield more power than people with guns. We can combat that isolation in students who feel disenfranchised and unprotected."

Evarts's work in her high school looks like very personalized reader's advisory. "Another subtle way to draw in these (and all) students is to work at remembering what individual students like to read. Most librarians do it anyway, but it's important to do it consciously. Students are flattered if you simply ask them how they liked a book that they're returning. You draw them in just by asking about the plot of a book that you haven't read yet." To reinforce her focus on relationships with students as readers, Evarts suggests that you allocate one school year's materials budget to focus on high-interest fiction, asking students for purchase requests and buying paperbacks to maximize the number of books you can purchase. "When you bulk up your fiction collection, they will come, isolated students among the others."

Among her easiest-to-implement suggestions, Evarts (2006) suggests you start a set of notecards headed with the names of students, listing titles that you think they might enjoy. "If a book arrives that you know a particular student will like, set it aside and make sure that she sees it when she comes to the library. Better yet, find out what class she's in and do a delivery." Such personalized attention to detail is certain to make any student feel special and their interests and needs validated.

One of Evarts's biggest triumphs involves giving students the option to use the library as a safe harbor. Because "lunch is one of the most stressful times for isolated students," Evarts looks for teens sitting alone in the dining hall to invite to her space instead. To counteract what she calls "the scariest place in any school," the cafeteria at lunchtime, Evarts opens her doors for students to bring their meals there. She said the accessibility of the space as a place to eat with proper garbage cans available actually eliminated earlier issues with discarded candy and food wrappers tucked behind books. Her child-first philosophy and open door during lunch were so radical and well received that they appeared in her hometown newspaper. "For kids who don't have a lot of friends, who don't like a ruckus, it can be a nice place," she said in that piece. "It's cleaner here than in the commons. It attracts a certain kind of kid. They realize it's not usual and they're pretty good" (Jensen 2004).

Gina Gomez, a high school junior, was one of the students who was in the Sauk Prairie library at lunchtime when the reporter visited. She emphasizes the affective aspects of the space. "This library is my home," she said. "I come here as much as I can—study hall, lunch. It's a place to relax. Miss Evarts makes it interesting. It's a whole lot calmer (than the commons)" (Jensen 2004).

Evarts and her principal Brian Salzer went on to speak to other education professionals about the benefits of allowing students to eat in the library, especially for isolated students. Evarts said some librarians told her it would be too messy or that their principals would never allow it. Salzer said of the library's success, "It's a climate Lynn Evarts has established" (Jensen 2004). I remember being absolutely thrilled when I moved to a second high school where I had an early conversation with the principal surrounding students eating in the library space. He asked whether or not this was something I was willing to allow. My response was that as long as the custodial staff would clean up properly, I had no problem with eating. A few students would take advantage of that opportunity to eat or work during lunch, but not the hordes I had worried would turn up with steaming trays of cafeteria food. For those who did come, it was often because they needed time or space to work away from the very social space that was the lunchroom.

OTHER INSPIRATIONAL LIBRARIANS

Evarts work is time-consuming, informed by deep local connections in her rural community, and she acknowledges that everyone has different levels of comfort in getting close to students, especially those with mental health issues. Another Midwestern school librarian who has done inspirational work on the supportive role of libraries is Meghan Harper, who is a part of the school library faculty at Kent State. When I met Harper, she was preparing for a series of Institute of Museum and Library Services (IMLS)-funded talks on "Opioids in Communities: Libraries in Response," presenting alongside journalist Sam Quinones (2015), author of the outstanding longform study of addiction and its effects on communities, *Dreamland: The True Tale of America's Opiate Epidemic*, winner of the National Book Critics Circle Award for General Nonfiction. Harper writes about resilience, the ethic of care in library settings, and countering the effects of intergenerational trauma in a project she calls Libraries Lending Hope. Her personal website features two outstanding annotated bibliographies on trauma-informed librarianship (Harper 2019).

When a student's past trauma is activated, the priority should be to keep them safe, stay calm, and get support as needed. Once a person's survival impulses kick in, they will not be able to reconnect to group norms or agreements until the body's survival response recalibrates. One option for increasing a feeling of sanctuary is using a smaller space like a closet or study as a "safe space" for students to remove themselves if needed to calm down. (Sprenger 2019). It is important that, after a needed time out, a child be able to return to a familiar setting and a sense of normalcy. "After the escalation has occurred, and the student and educator's nervous systems have reregulated, it is critical to invest time with student and community members to reconnect, restore relationship, and learn from what took place," writes Larry Ferlazzo (2019). "Trauma is a fact of life, but it is not a life sentence. Trauma heals through safety, connection, and slowly rewiring the brain to slow down the survival response. Focus on resilience and build it into your curriculum."

Another prominent school librarian working in the affective and emotional area is Anita Cellucci, a Library Journal Mover and Shaker, past president of the Massachusetts Library Association, and member of the American Association of School Libraries Board of Directors. On Twitter, she's known as "@theempatheticlibrarian," and she has been presenting on mental health supports for students. Her work at Westborough High School is inspirational if you're interested in ways to build these communities of care in your schools.

EMPATHY

School librarians must model empathy ourselves, which is easier said than done in the current political polarized climate. In October of 2019, the head of teen services from a major public library published a column on self-care in the online edition of *School Library Journal* (*SLJ*), detailing her very personal experience with postpartum depression and burnout. It was received with a rabid and instantaneous chorus of criticism, most validly that the librarian did not seek professional help but instead emphasized self-care, which many readers saw was excusing her employer for abdicating the responsibility for employee well-being by shifting that burden onto the employee themselves. I understand that criticism of the workplace emphasis on wellness occurring after hours, but I don't believe that the conditions of any job are likely to change under our current economic realities. But another point of contention was the "before and after" photographs the librarian included in her piece, demonstrating her improved fitness and weight loss. Some readers believed it was not body positive and harkened to juxtapositions most common in weight loss advertisements. The expressions on that librarian's face were more telling than anything— she had been unhappy and now she was clearly happier.

My own reaction to the piece, which I had bookmarked to read later and was surprised to find had been taken down upon reconsideration as not having met *SLJ* editorial guidelines, was much more positive. I did not see it as fat-shaming, but focusing on strength and wellness, and found the strategies she had adopted seem to me the marks of healthy adjustment to a high-pressure job and the complexities of motherhood as well as other personal concerns. This was one woman's journey, and she obviously felt better than she had and was willing to share what was a deeply personal transformation. The whole backlash demonstrated a lack of empathy on the part of the readers who had been so vocal in their criticism. I was discouraged that a mob mentality had eliminated what was a potentially helpful piece of practical sharing from someone within the profession—did we really have so little patience to listen to other's points of view and lived experience? It seemed antithetical to our professional ethos and any ethic of care.

Everyone is fighting their own battle. In the midst of "cancel culture" and performative shaming enabled by social media, school libraries need to be accepting places. As long as our students do not hurt each other or themselves, emotionally or physically, it is not just worthwhile but imperative we showcase a range of viewpoints and experiences. Justice Brennan called the school library a laboratory for intellectual freedom, and that is not limited to academics, but lifestyles as well. If this librarian had been a student of mine, I would have cheered along with her when she ran a 5K. I was deeply disappointed with how many of my colleagues would choose to lash out at someone sharing in such an open and candid way.

We all have our own inspirations for our practice, and many of those demonstrate that the library can be the soul of the school and a critical resource for the students who need it most.

REFERENCES

Evarts, Lynne. 2006. "The Library as Sanctuary." *VOYA*. December 2006. 404–406.

Ferlazzo, Larry. 2019. "Classroom Q&A: A 'Trauma-Informed Classroom Is a Safe and Secure Place.'" *Education Week*. March 21, 2019. http://blogs.edweek.org/teachers/classroom_qa_with_larry _ferlazzo/2019/05/response_a_trauma_informed_classroom_is _a_safe_and_secure_place.html.

Harper, Meghan. 2019. http://www.meghanharper.org/

Jensen, Kirsten. 2004. "A Place to Be Yourself." *Sauk Prairie Eagle*. March 24, 2004.

Quinones, Sam. 2015. *Dreamland: The True Tale of America's Opiate Epidemic*. New York: Bloomsbury.

Sprenger, Marilee. 2019. "The Break-Up Letter: Bring SEL Alive in Class." *Middleweb*. April 14, 2019. https://www.middleweb.com /40116/the-break-up-letter-bring-sel-alive-in-class/.

NINE

Bibliotherapy

The association of reading material and moral outcomes has a long history. The inherent belief that reading material influences young minds is visible in the heavy didacticism of early fairy tales and moral tracts. In the nineteenth century, novel reading was largely derided wholesale, and the mid-twentieth-century panic around comic books and juvenile delinquency was a more recent manifestations of the impulse to restrict young people's media consumption. Today, we might express concern about "screen time," but what that often masks are misgivings about the media itself. Nowhere is this idea that young people will be influenced by books more manifest than in the American Library Association's annual list of most-challenged titles, so many of which are authored for young people. Despite the need for reading practice demanding quantity rather than quality of text consumption, school librarians are still fighting battles around age-appropriate literature and its fitness for young people.

THE BIBLIOTHERAPY CONCEPT

A belief in the power of the written word is manifest in the bibliotherapy movement. That term bibliotherapy can be traced to the minister Samuel Crothers (1917), who wrote a 1916 pamphlet about expanding the practice of psychotherapy to include recommendations of literature as "a stock of thoughts in such a variety of forms that they can be used not only for food but for medicine" (p. 4). His doctor character suggests "don't pay attention to the purely literary or historical classifications. I don't care whether a book is ancient or modern, whether it is English or German, whether it is prose or verse" (p. 4), writing that "a book may be a stimulant or a sedative or an irritant or a soporific" (p. 5). Crothers goes on to speculate that there are fashions in literature, like romantic emulation of Byron, and proscribes escapism as a cure for stress: "In cases where the conscience has been overstimulated by incessant modern demands, I find Trollope a sovereign remedy" (p. 19).

Crothers's model would find resonance in hospitals caring for the wounded recuperating from the First World War. The library services established for the duration of the war were quickly adapted to serve the returning servicemen and stressed a scientific approach to bibliotherapy akin to occupational therapy. The sick were believed to be receptive to reading and were considered to be in a position to cultivate the patience necessary to appreciate great works of literature.

Though bibliotherapy as a term can be considered a "sort of stupid American word," it represents the attempts to systematize reading recommendations (Mahoney, 2019). Mary M. Mahoney, a historian of bibliotherapy, said the efforts to position bibliotherapy as scientific echo Freud's contemporary anxieties that his own work read too much like short fiction and lacked the necessary science to be taken seriously (2017). These early efforts were also punctuated with warnings about the danger of unmediated access to books (Downey 1934), something that echoes even today in youth services departments.

Interwar accounts of bibliotherapy support the promotion of the intellectual, moral, and improving power of literature, with recommendations along the lines that biography and travel "have places" in hospital libraries and that given the "suggestibility" of those recovering, political propaganda should be banned. In 1944, bibliotherapeutic librarian Ruth Tews wrote about "case histories of patient reading," marking an interest in fashion magazine as a positive sign because it could be equated to the "patient taking an interest in her appearance."

Among the pioneers of bibliotherapy was Sadie P. Delaney, head of the Veteran's Administration libraries. "Delaney saw her library as a tool for correcting the injustices of a segregated, unequal society," as she refined her practice as chief librarian at the Veterans' Hospital in Tuskegee, Alabama, in the 1920s (Palmieri 2016). Her efforts were often modeled, including "getting to know patients on an individual basis and recommending books to them, creating circulation lists and pamphlets, holding a weekly radio talk, and establishing book clubs and other activities to connect readers with one another" (Palmieri 2016). Many of those strategies for reading promotion would not be out of place in today's school libraries.

More than a century later, the bibliotherapeutic trend reemerged in a *New York Times* column by Lori Gottlieb. She presents fiction in particular as a tool for seeing situations in relief. "If, for instance, someone has problematic relationships but either can't see her patterns clearly or would feel ashamed acknowledging them directly, I'll often suggest a novel or memoir rather than a self-help book that addresses these issues head on" (Gottlieb 2019).

School librarians know that students of all ages need to be exposed to a variety of text to become fluent readers.

FROM MIRRORS TO PRISMS

In children's services, bibliotherapy can be seen at the heart of Rudine Sims Bishop's (1990) description of literature as "mirrors, windows, and sliding glass doors." In schools, we have those students who want to see their own lives reflected, the mirrors providing the "self-affirmation" that Sims Bishop (1990) esteems: "When children cannot see themselves reflected in the books they read, or when the images they see are distorted, negative, or laughable, they learn a powerful lesson about how they are devalued in the society of which they are a part." In my own work, I remember a student asking, *sotto voce*, why there weren't any books about girls who had babies. I instinctively mentioned a couple of titles, but she clarified that she wanted a romance. She wanted to feel that she, a young mother, was worthy of love and had a glimmer of hope that she would find someone who would cherish her and her baby. I also had several students tell me that too many of the books about African Americans were urban stories; these did not reflect their own identities as rural Southerners.

Windows are necessary to build empathy for others, and Sims Bishop (1990) says that even children who are from majority groups "suffer from a lack of availability of books about others." In addition to the range of traditions and values important to different social groups, she uses the example of exposure to a range of language, "From reading, children can become aware of some of the many variations in the way English is spoken in this country, and the richness those variations add to language." Though Sims Bishop does not fully explore the metaphor of sliding glass doors, the role of reading in that context becomes apparent when one considers the number of individuals who read somewhat aspirationally, be it about rarified careers, different geographic locales, or in an immersive world, be it historical, fantastic, or dystopian. The ability to realize one's own efficacy is embedded in the that sliding door concept.

Uma Krishnaswami (2019) pushes Sims Bishop's model one step further, calling for "prisms" for reading, saying that "diverse texts, like glass, are capable of operating in complex ways," to "disrupt and challenge ideas about diversity through multifaceted and intersecting identities, settings, cultural contexts, and histories." This is an apt metaphor when considering how to promote a range of literature beyond that reflected in local school demographics. Because global awareness is increasingly important, international children's books in particular deserve a wider readership.

BROADER READING PROMOTION IN SCHOOLS

While mindful library collections will reflect student interests and reader driven acquisitions, it is incumbent on the school librarian to acquire and promote a broad range of materials. This has been framed as reading wildly, reading across borders, or summer reading "bingo" reflecting the wide range of genres and literature available. Consider how you pick and showcase the best exemplars of each sort of book and have them available and intermingled with more popular titles. And know that, through accessible display and other relatively low-effort passive reader's advisory activities, you can normalize a range of human experience. When you include an LGBTQ story alongside romance, or historical fiction from a range of points of view, you are expanding the acknowledged universe for your students.

Many current trends try to divide the reading experience to make location reading materials easier. I would resist this, challenging the librarian instead to know their collections and add access points to their materials in ways that make their catalog more useful. Genrefication of school library collections promotes more narrow finding, and through that, more narrow reading and, I believe, most categories are so idiosyncratically assigned that they should be avoided in favor of the broader collection designations students are more likely to encounter in public libraries.

Consider Delaney's early bibliotherapeutic efforts to connect readers to each other. Some of the best conversations I have experienced around literature have come through the NEH's The Big Read program, which our local public library was sure to involve high schools, and whole-grade reads. One easy way to make reading social and concurrently increase circulation involves holding multiple copies of the same edition of a book. For younger girls, the idea of reading alongside a friend is compelling, and the resulting conversations can be harnessed to create a circle of readers. Other ways to build a student-centered reading culture involve asking students to guest-curate displays with their own favorites. Paper tents can provide shelf-talking recommendations for fans of particular titles. And don't overlook the faculty and staff as reading influencers. At one school where I worked, we used the ALA READ poster software to share teachers photographed with their favorite books, which were then prominently available for checkout. Another recommendation stream can come from snapshots of students "caught reading" on campus.

Bibliotherapy can expand out to create a vibrant literacy experience for students who encounter a range of text, building fluency and stamina that will serve them well when they encounter "cold reads" on standardized tests, and inculcate broader background knowledge and preparation for citizenship. These are, after all, the most aspirational goals of school librarianship, the sliding glass door to the future we seek to provide.

REFERENCES

Bishop, Rudine Sims. 1990. "Mirrors, Windows, and Sliding Glass Doors." *Perspectives: Choosing and Using Books for the Classroom* 6, no. 3 (Summer): ix–xi.

Crothers, Samuel McChord. 1917. *A Literary Clinic.* Boston, MA: Houghton Mifflin. https://www.google.com/books/edition/A_Literary _Clinic/molJAAAAYAAJ?hl=en&gbpv=0.

Downey, Fairfax. 1932. "She Takes Her Patient's Literary Pulse." *American Magazine* 344 (April): 71–72.

Gottlieb, Lori. 2019. "Your Therapist's Prescription? The Right Book." *The New York Times.* July 26, 2019. https://www.nytimes.com /2019/07/26/books/review/can-a-book-cure-mental-illness.html.

Krishnaswami, Uma. 2019. "Why Stop at Windows and Mirrors?: Children's Book Prisms." *The Horn Book.* January 17, 2019. https:// www.hbook.com/?detailStory=why-stop-at-windows-and-mirrors -childrens-book-prisms.

Mahoney, Mary M. 2017. "The Library as Medicine Cabinet: Inventing Bibliotherapy in the Interwar Period." In *Libraries: Traditions and*

Innovations. Papers from the Library History Seminar XIII, edited by Melanie A. Kimball and Katherine E. Wisser. Munich: K G Saur Verlag Gmbh & Co.

Mahoney, Mary M. 2019. "Americans Playing at Science: Imagining Bibliotherapy and Its Uses in a Modern Hospital." Society for the History of Authorship, Readership and Publishing Presentation. Amherst, MA. July 18, 2019.

Palmieri, Brooke. 2016. "Sadie P. Delaney: Our Lady of Bibliotherapy." *Journal of the History of Ideas*. March 21, 2016. https://jhiblog.org/2016/03/21/sadie-p-delaney-our-lady-of-bibliotherapy/.

Tews, Ruth. 1944. "Case Histories of Patients' Reading." *Library Journal* 69: 484–487.

TEN

Connections to Social Services

WHEN TO SEEK HELP

There are many times when the needs of students and teachers will be outside your purview. Librarians are, by nature, connectors. Without exception, we want people to have the resources to make their lives easier and better, and we want to reduce the friction in getting people whatever we need. As discussed, by limiting your own stress response and streamlining your productivity, you can cultivate additional mental capacities to make powerful connections between individuals, organizations, and other resources in your school, community, and beyond at the point of need.

WHOLE PERSON LIBRARIANSHIP: SOCIAL WORK CONCEPTS FOR HOLISTIC PATRON SERVICES

Nienow and Zettervall (2019) evolved Whole Person Librarianship as a movement to apply social work concepts to library practice to improve patron services. Their assertion is that all librarians can learn to provide more holistic service by applying tools and techniques grounded in counseling and social work practice to bolster mental health, self-care, and understanding of and working with students in crisis. One social work concept they outline with applicability to libraries is the situation of person-in-environment, which stresses the importance of understanding an individual and their behavior in light of the environmental contexts in which that person lives and acts. A related practice is cultural humility, an ongoing process to encourage self-awareness of personal and cultural biases as well as awareness and sensitivity to significant cultural issues of others. We have come to accept cultural competence as an element of public service library work, but often still privilege certain community behaviors. Nienow and Zettervall draw upon the social work literature to challenge that positioning.

Asset mapping, the process of identifying valuable resources in your community, is another exercise with roots in social work that can be valuable as your work with children. There are going to be many times when students will require help that is outside your bailiwick. But children in crisis want to have the sense that adults know what to do. Avoid uncertainty by educating yourself on resources available beforehand. I remember a new assistant principal from another state promising a family English Language Learner support at a school where there was none, and, in my state, the conversational introduction of tools that could help students makes the system subsequently responsible for providing them. I have heard teachers of special education discuss ways to lead parents to the conclusion that their child might need new glasses or assistive technology. If the parent raises the issue, the school system would not be responsible for the cost of these items, as they were not introduced as a necessary component of a free and appropriate public education.

At the very least, have some general knowledge about local agencies and services related to mental health, emergency medicine, social support, child welfare, alternative school settings, and support groups for those with addictions or those with family members coping with addictions. Because school librarians have the mandate to report physical and sexual abuse, many of us have received training and protocols related to those issues. But work with your administration and guidance staff to know the best routes for helping young people in your community.

WORKING WITH OTHER LIBRARIES

One of the first things a new school librarian should do is get to know the other librarians. First and foremost, you will be working closely with the area's feeder schools, if it is a high school or middle school, or the schools where your students will feed, if you were at the elementary or primary levels. It is also critical that school librarians get in contact with the local youth services librarian, or in smaller communities, the local public library director. These colleagues will prove to be invaluable resources as you tailor your program and facility to the needs of the individuals in your community, and open lines of communications will benefit you both. Again, this goes back to the key points of intentionality and articulation. Once you know what your teachers and students need, you can seek those resources from other partner institutions. And serendipity is an element of this collegiality. Perhaps it's knowing that an exhibit at a local university will inform social science fair projects, or the policies related to public library cards in the community.

As scary as change can be, partnerships can be even scarier, especially when the rhetoric supporting such cooperation is around pooling resources and reducing redundancy. No public library can replace the school library, and no school library can replace a local public library. But there have been instances where the two library types have been able to partner for economies of scale. In my own home state, our collection of state funded databases, the Alabama Virtual Library, is an example of school, university, and public librarians coming together to envision, enact, sustain, promote, and enculturate all citizens with ubiquitous high-quality information resources. The latest incarnations of the virtual library do not even require associated possession of a public library card, instead depending upon geo-authentication for verification of subscription access for every person in the state. This is a radical interpretation of provision of information as a right of the citizenry. The partnership between Nashville Public Libraries in the local school system known as Limitless Libraries is it another terrific example of a public library sharing its resources, increasing usage and service by adding schools to their routing stops. Students all have cards and can request materials to be delivered to their local school; teachers are allowed to check out an unlimited amount of materials.

It can be remarkable what other librarians are willing to do for you and your students. Some systems will allow you to set up a fine-free Interlibrary Loan account for your school library. And when you are returning materials you have borrowed for school, just mentioning that you are a school librarian might get your overdue fines waived. Too many school librarians worry that they are burdening the busy public librarians. But, in reaching out to school librarians, too many public librarians try to replicate the hierarchy of public libraries and go through the principal of the school. Public school principals tend to deflect most outside inquiries from their staff, so odds are slim those requests may even reach school librarians. My suggestion is that school librarians be vocal about your professional role when working with public library staff as well as professional colleagues. You need to position yourself as an uber-user of the public library.

When one high school where I worked created a ninth-grade academy, that concentration of students provided easy access for local public librarians wanting to promote summer reading. This became a regular partnership. They were also able to sign up all interested ninth graders in one fell swoop. In return, I was asked to sit on a grant committee that enabled my school community access to a range of free health resources. It was a win-win.

WORKING WITH COUNSELING STAFF

Along with showcasing empathy, school libraries can normalize the experience of seeking help, be that within the school or without. There are a range of excellent books that model counseling skills at the school and professional levels, and sharing our own experiences can be meaningful. Talk therapy can be productive, but just as important as opening yourself up to that experience is finding the right person to work with, something that I think is not emphasized enough. I have attempted counseling several times, but only once with any success, finding someone with whom I could connect and communicate. I still use many of the analogies that therapist shared with me on a regular basis. If I had not had that experience, I might not be able to champion professional support as potentially valuable.

Lynne Evarts wrote, in providing sanctuary for students, "Another ally within your school building is your counseling department. School counselors might give you background information about a particular student (without breach of confidentiality) or help the student with a specific issue. Because isolated students are often hesitant to reach out to strangers, it might be helpful for you to make the initial contact or accompany the student to the counselor's office" (2006).

School counselors, like school librarians, may or may not have had classroom experience. I found that any time spent teaching really colors the way that a counselor approaches their job. Counselors who have worked for other youth agencies tend to take a whole child approach and seem more likely to extend their role to provision students with supplies, clothes, and food. School counselors coming from the classroom are more likely to focus on building level test coordination and administration and handling individual student discipline in behavioral issues the myriad other things that school counselors get involved with carrying out. At some high schools there might be a dedicated counselor working on college admissions. At other schools, working with expectant and new mothers might demand special designation in the counseling staff. It is important to determine the priorities of the guidance staff at your school. In some communities, their role will involve a lot of enrichment and out of school opportunities. The counselor might work hand-in-hand with social services and law enforcement at the city county or district level. But whatever the structural and operational focus of the guidance counseling staff in your building it is critical that you communicate with them about how you can support students. We both have the same goals in terms of supporting and empowering young people. By combining your efforts in energy with the guidance staff you can shift your school culture from reactive constructive and embed valuable social emotional learning.

I still remember the time a guidance counselor called with a question. She had a student who was with her, and they were talking about careers, and if it could possibly be true that you would need to get a master's degree to be a librarian. I affirmed that graduate school was required, dumbstruck that I worked with someone whose very position involved knowledge of career preparation, yet who lacked a fundamental understanding of my job.

I have seen many elementary schools where school librarians were working in concert with counselors so that both specialists are essentially reinforcing the same aspects of social emotional learning. One easy shift of benefit to all learners is to work to improve the literature used by counseling staff. In my experience, counselors love the entire oeuvre of Amy Krouse Rosenthal, and the American Psychological Society's Magination Press imprint. You can also involve the counseling staff by leveraging their expertise to create a collection of information about college admissions and standardized test prep guides—always one of the hottest titles in high school libraries.

WORKING WITH COLLEGE ADMISSIONS

One thing many members of the faculty might not realize are the amount of meetings that take place within the library space, all of which must be managed with public-facing effort. The library is a go-to whenever anyone needs to have a confidential conversation in a quiet corner. If you work with high school students, you'll organize, actively or passively, college recruiters and university representatives checking with potential applicants for recruits. Don't be shy about asking for pencils, pens and other branded swag that you can distribute to students. If your school has feeder programs into college athletics it is worth knowing the National College Athletic Association (NCAA) eligibility guidelines and stressing those to students who counselors might be less aware are interested in sports at that level. And now that gaming is an intercollegiate sport, more library regulars may be going on to compete in that arena.

Too few school librarians consider their role in college readiness. Visits from university admissions officers provide an organic opportunity to talk about the college library transition, too. Since our database consortium will remain accessible for students staying in-state, it is worth reinforcing their value, citation generation, and plagiarism detection tools like TurnI-tIn. You might also demonstrate Library of Congree (LC) classifications through a local university catalog. Students might not realize that they have access to local public libraries in their college towns, so it is worth reinforcing for access to leisure reading. No student should be flummoxed when encountering a different classification system on campus.

WORKING WITH MILITARY RECRUITING

As with college representatives who want your students to continue their education on their campuses, depending on your school demographic, you may have military recruiters looking for a quiet corner to have a conversation with students about their future prospects. Depending on your personal feelings about militarization and endless war, this can be difficult, especially for school librarians who have had former students killed in conflict.

Interactions with military recruiters will vary based on your community and administration. At many public schools, the ASVAB (the Armed Services Vocational Aptitude Battery) is a mandatory standardized test that provides information about your abilities for military leverage. In my own high school days, I remember the scuttlebutt being to do poorly on the ASVAB unless you wanted to be dogged by calls from the military. At my first school, there was a robust Junior Reserve Officer Training Corps (JROTC) program and a revolving cast of recruiters on campus. Those cadets were among some of the most regular users of the library, making weekly trips to check out independent reading. At the other high school where I worked, JROTC was treated as a vocational program and was conducted off-campus; only students who either expressed an interest in particular careers or were enrolled in the JROTC program took the ASVAB in that setting. One of my favorite students was a cadet who won state-level sharpshooting competitions and planned a military career using those particular skills, but she couldn't withstand the stress of basic training and returned home to work a retail job. She is one student who I wish that I had pushed to cultivate other interests.

Working in a rural area, I saw how military service could sometimes be a springboard for young people uncertain of taking the next step, as well as the tremendous benefits of attending the military academies. There were dedicated recruiters who worked on fitness with students in small groups to make sure they met physical requirements and genuinely demonstrated an interest in our student's lives and well-being beyond cannon fodder. At the same time, I could see how most recruits were unlikely to ever access the educational benefits described. But seeing former students return to the community with experience through international travel, often returning to responsible positions in the community like law enforcement and teaching, I began to consider it a viable path for our students.

I would take a note from the public library and consider the school library space to be a public forum and provide the same small group with one-on-one access and support as you would when accommodating visitors working with expectant mothers or developing readers.

OTHER LOCAL AGENCIES

If you are working in a secondary school, even with the ubiquity of directory information available online, health information is one area where I would consider sticking to an analog format and having contact information for Planned Parenthood and the state public health department as well as any other local agencies. You may never need to pass it along, but if you do, you do not want to leave an electronic trail. Think of this as a contemporary version of the vertical file.

SELF-CARE

Self-care for librarians is a hot topic at the moment. A panel on the topic at ALA Annual 2019 drew a standing-room-only audience. There have been vocal and visible challenges to the implicit obligations placed upon librarians to do unpaid emotional labor. *Vocational awe* is a term coined by Fobazi Ettarh (2017) representing "the idea that libraries as institutions are inherently good. It assumes that some or all core aspects of the profession are beyond critique, and it, in turn, underpins many librarians' sense of identity and emotional investment in the profession." Ettarh's critique of the implicit culture of libraries and librarians found great resonance in the profession.

I have begun to worry when I interview a potential school library student and they say that reading is their hobby. When your work and your leisure activity are indistinguishable, it sets you up for poor work-life balance. Instead, I would rather they spend time on themselves.

"It's important to separate your work life and home life," wrote Price (2019). "If the two become too enmeshed, it can be highly stressful. Try not checking your work email when you're home, and read books for pleasure, not research. Even better, try finding a hobby that has absolutely nothing to do with the library."

"Self-care became my hobby," reported librarian Kathleen Houlihan, Teen Central Manager at the Austin Public Library, during a YALSA webinar on professional resilience, outlining how her own concerted efforts improved her health and well-being (2019). Social media can exacerbate stress, especially when it focuses on issues of social justice. Williams and Delapp (2016) assert that "repeated exposure to images and accounts of racial violence can trigger the same symptoms as PTSD."

LIBRARIAN'S STRESS AND BURNOUT

A 2018 survey found some 94 percent of workers report feeling stress at work, and almost a third say their stress level is high to unsustainably high. Elevated stress levels not only impact work productivity, but also affect employees' personal lives (Hansen 2018). Library work, like teaching, is unusual in that it is simultaneously affective, intellectual, and physical. School librarians are among those who work "at small libraries in particular (and) are at risk for burning out, as all of the responsibilities of the library often weigh on one person's shoulders" (Price 2019). In studies of librarian stress, the pressure that librarians place on themselves is emphasized (Larrivee 2014). The librarian role involves a range of display rules, expressing a range of emotions and interventions based on audience, depending on each group's norms, which define how and in what manner emotions and thoughts are acceptably expressed. All of this can be exhausting.

Few outside the profession realize the range of roles a school librarian embodies over the day. It is rewarding work, but one that can take a psychic toll. "To work in a library I also had to be a social worker and a first responder, an advocate for the underserved, and a human with very thick skin," wrote Amanda Oliver in a *Los Angeles Times* opinion piece about librarians experiencing PTSD (2019). It will always be necessary to distribute the responsibilities for your students' health and welfare; not doing so is a recipe for burnout.

Professional burnout is phenomenon that represents emotional exhaustion, depersonalization, and low professional efficacy, first define by Maslach in 1981. Burnout research had its roots in caregiving and service occupations, in which the core of the job was the relationship between provider and recipient. A burnout-like syndrome was mentioned in the Old Testament, as the prophet Elijah was plunged into deep despair, longing for death and wishing to fall into a deep sleep (Kings I, New International Version, 19:3-4). Burnout is not just being tired, it can actually alter neural circuits in the brain, "changes may be responsible for the inability of those experiencing high degrees of burnout to adequately regulate their emotions, a decrease in fine motor function, and diminished ability to shift from one stimulus to another" (Maslach and Jackson 1981).

Christian offers many recommendations to combat librarian burnout, including better integrating the ideas of "emotional labor," emotional intelligence, and burnout in library science program curricula. "Library schools and workplace training ordinarily do not address issues involving emotion at work, and therefore do not prepare library students and staff for associated problems in the field. A librarian's professional development should reflect an understanding of emotional labor, skilled relationship building techniques, and an acquired emotional intelligence" (Christian 2015).

Broadly, emotional intelligence encompasses reading moods, behaviors, and motives from a range of individuals and includes awareness, self-regulation, and an appreciation of group dynamics. These skills improve the quality of relationship building by appreciating the way people feel and adjusting your responses accordingly. Mindfulness feeds emotional intelligence. "If teachers can use mindfulness practice to create metacognitive distance, they can take their ego out of interactions with students" (Schwartz 2019).

In 2001, *School Librarian's Workshop* published a short series of three reports on a survey examining sources of stress in school libraries. The results are not out-of-step with today's concerns. Among the findings was that old and outdated technology equipment was reported to be a chief problem for librarians, in addition to dealing struggling with physical plant maintenance issues. Working with teachers, but not students, proved stressful, as did work assignments outside the library (School Librarian's Workshop 2001). In another study of librarian stress, emotional exhaustion was negatively associated with "autonomy, role clarity, coworker support, and recovery experiences of relaxation, mastery, and control" (Salyers, Watkins, and Painter 2018). Too many librarians do not reflect on the source of their workplace stress, but seeing factors others have outlined can be helpful as identifying the problems can help you address them at the root rather than treating the symptom.

As professionals so often working alone with little understanding of our concerns and stresses, it is critical that we build supportive networks outside the building that we can turn to for advice and support. Professional organizations are a good place to start, but local colleagues will have a better appreciation of your budget and facilities concerns and local culture. "Trying to do everything yourself is a surefire way to get burned out," wrote Price. "We must remember that we have library assistants for a reason, and it's literally their job to help." With the realities of school libraries today, such paraprofessional assistance is not always a given. "Even if you don't have a library assistant, there are likely many people in town who would be happy to help with summer reading or big events. If you feel stressed out by an upcoming program, find someone to help you plan and set up—don't be a hero! It benefits your library and community when you don't bear every burden and end up stressed and sweating at every event" (Price 2019). I would add that we need to focus on volunteers who are truly helpful rather than politically advisable and be ruthless in rejecting any help that will create more work for us in our libraries in terms of supervision and oversight. Many times, parent volunteers can be more interested in the social lives of students and inter-school politics than in providing real help. I know that when my paraprofessional aide was out, instructing substitutes in the aspects of her job like shelf-reading and reshelving not only took up considerably more time than if I had carried those out myself but also resulted in confusion when the tasks were not carried our properly.

There is a growing teacher shortage in most areas of the United States, as retirements couple with low recruitment based on limited earning expectations. It is almost always more worthwhile to keep an employee rather than replace them. I often hear from Instructional Leadership colleagues the urban legend that school librarians never move buildings or retire, meaning that administrators could have less reason to address their concerns. I anticipate that, as changing teaching demographics and temporary educators become more commonplace, school leaders will be forced to provide more support for their faculties. "Given the negative effects that burnout has on job performance, attendance, personal and professional relationships, and healthcare costs, it would be to organizations' advantage to implement burnout mitigation plans," Nardine (2019) wrote. "These plans can, in turn, decrease costs associated with rapid employee turnover and significant absence due to illness, increase cohesive work toward overarching goals of both library and institution, and demonstrate employees' value to the organization, thus creating a positive feedback loop." The main issue in school settings is that, given the small size of most faculties and lack of resources available to public institutions, it will be difficult for any mitigation plan to address all the potential needs of faculty and staff, and it is normal for any efforts to be more student-centered.

Much of the increased reckoning with self-care and burnout is generational. Millennial Americans are not reluctant about expressing their mental health needs, so employers will be less able to pretend that mental health is not really a workplace concern. When you couple this with both security concerns related to mass public and school shootings and the divisive political climate of our time, it is incumbent upon our schools to provide supports for social and emotional learning for the faculty and staff as well as students. By embracing reflection and mindfulness in all aspects of our working life, we are taking charge of our own well-being and resisting the pace of an always-on imperative. And, in modeling these practices, we demonstrate a range of healthy behaviors for students to emulate.

REFERENCES

Christian, Linda A. 2015 "A Passion Deficit: Occupational Burnout and the New Librarian: A Recommendation Report." *The Southeastern Librarian* 62: 4. https://digitalcommons.kennesaw.edu/seln/vol62 /iss4/2.

Ettarh, Fobazi. 2017. "Vocational Awe?" May 30, 2017. https://fobaziettarh .wordpress.com/2017/05/30/vocational-awe/.

Evarts, Lynne. 2006. "The Library as Sanctuary." *VOYA*. December 2006. 404–406.

Hansen, Brianna. 2018. "Crash and Burnout: Is Workplace Stress the New Normal?" *Wrike*. September 6, 2018. https://www.wrike.com/blog /stress-epidemic-report-announcement/.

Houlihan, Kathleen. 2019. "The Resilient Librarian Workbook: Cracking Your Self-Care Code." YALSA Webinar Companion Materials. August 8, 2019. http://www.ala.org/yalsa/webinars/webinarson demand-date.

Kings I, New International Version, Bible Gateway, 19:3-4. https://www .biblegateway.com/passage/?search=1+Kings+19&version=NIV.

Larrivee, Anne. 2014. "Exploring the Stressors of New Librarians." *Library Scholarship*. 1. https://orb.binghamton.edu/librarian_fac/1.

Maslach, C., and S. E. Jackson. 1981. "The Measurement of Experienced Burnout." *Journal of Occupational Behavior 2*, no. 2: 99–113. https://doi.org/10.1002/job.4030020205.

Nardine, Jennifer. 2019. "The State of Academic Liaison Librarian Burnout in ARL Libraries in the United States." *College and Resource Libraries* 80:4. https://crl.acrl.org/index.php/crl/article/view/17398 /19176.

Nienow, Mary C., and Sara K. Zettervall. 2019. *Whole Person Librarianship: A Social Work Approach to Patron Services*. Santa Barbara, CA: Libraries Unlimited.

Oliver, Amanda. 2019. "Working as a Librarian Gave Me Post-Traumatic Stress Disorder Symptoms." *Los Angeles Times*. April 19, 2019. https://www.latimes.com/opinion/op-ed/la-oe-oliver-librarian-the -public-movie-20190419-story.html.

Price, Chelsea. 2019. "When Programming Isn't Fun Anymore: Fighting Job Burnout." Programming Librarian. June 13, 2019. http://www .programminglibrarian.org/blog/when-programming-isn%E2% 80%99t-fun-anymore-fighting-job-burnout.

Salyers, Michelle P., Melanie A. Watkins, and Amber Painter. 2018. "Predictors of Burnout in Public Library Employees." *Journal of Library and Information Science* 51, no. 4 (February 21): 974–983. https://doi.org/10.1177/0961000618759415.

The School Librarian's Workshop (SLW). 2001. "Tracking the Trends: Sources of Stress Survey Results." 22, no. 1: 2–3.

Schwartz, Katrina. 2019. "Why Mindfulness and Trauma-Informed Teaching Don't Always Go Together." KQED Mindshift. January 27, 2019. https://www.kqed.org/mindshift/52881/why-mindfulness -and-trauma-informed-teaching-dont-always-go-together.

Williams, Monnica, and Ryan Delapp. 2016. "Tuning Out." Slate. July 14, 2016. https://slate.com/technology/2016/07/when-racial-violence -happens-its-just-as-important-to-tune-out-as-it-is-to-tune-in.html.

ELEVEN

Mindfulness in Difficult Times

Be it a national emergency like a pandemic or large-scale terrorist attack, or a more localized tragedy like the death of a teacher or classmate, there will always be mental and emotional challenges for young people to work through. A culture of mindfulness enables mental and emotional training for resilience in difficult times, minimizes panic responses, and promotes creative solutions to personal and societal problems.

In times of crisis, the impulse to protect students from the most negative aspects of the real world can be a knee-jerk one, especially for those adults who have dedicated their careers to helping young people. But communicating hard realities is an important part of the educational process, be it in school or at home. Even the youngest children can learn to first identify and then sit with uncomfortable and unusual emotions, part of understanding that these are transitory states and that they do not have to be reactive or respond impulsively.

Talking about mental health issues and validating concerns of young people is of paramount importance given the stresses of modern life. For students in schools and classrooms that promote regular practice in naming feelings and having those supported, it will be easier to draw on inner resources cultivated in more normal times, where stress was more likely to be interpersonal than societal. Comforting students is easier when they have become able to identify what helps and calms them personally, and the ability, time and space to self-soothe are incorporated into the culture. In cases where students have needed to work through grief and loss, the most empathetic classroom teachers often ditch lesson plans in favor of talking circles, promoting sharing in small groups or whole classes or offering time and space for students to create art or writing. Creative activities can be cathartic and allow students to process their emotions, and can sometime produce meaningful products to share with grieving families. Teachers and librarians can mirror the range of student feelings and lend validation to both the emotions and process of working through them, modeling the competencies of social-emotional learning.

SOCIAL—BUT NOT EMOTIONAL—DISTANCING

In March 2020, schools were suspended in most states due to the COVID-19 outbreak. Initially, there was terrific concern that educational attainment not be disrupted, though that abated somewhat when it was announced that, nationally, standardized assessments used for accountability, which can be stressful in the best of times, would not be required because of the emergency.

Many school systems struggled with the necessity of keeping children fed as a foundational precursor to keeping them learning. School administrators and teachers provided, and even delivered, supplies for families they knew to be food-insecure. But, across the demographic split of professional families who are able to work from home and those parents whose service industry jobs either dictated they still report to work or who were laid off because of closures associated with advised social distancing or orders to shelter in place, household disruption was widespread. There are many children who were left to their own devices, amid a firehose of community panic, or neglected in light of more immediate parental concerns.

The department of education in my state cautioned that instruction could not seamlessly shift online for several reasons. One of those involved the uneven provision of wireless connectivity, though some districts tried to counter this, either through the provision of wireless hot spots or promoting partnerships with Internet providers that offered discounted access (though when this was limited to families who were not in arrears with those companies and that disqualified many of the neediest households). But for students in rural areas, mobile signals can be nonexistent, making these mechanisms unworkable, and even in areas with fiber optic networks, online services slowed their streaming bitrates considerably, amid predictions that all the work from home would break the internet, making video and teleconferencing sub-optimal experiences.

The other equity aspect school leaders emphasized during the school closure was the need for accessibility for students receiving support services, cautioning that if special needs and language learner integration were not provided, then districts were effectively opening themselves up to a lawsuit by not ensuring a free and appropriate public education for all.

With these considerations in place, even teachers in districts with 1:1 technology initiatives went back to duplicating worksheets and other paper-based activities that could be disseminated in hard copies when necessary. Teachers knew that these were superficial practices, the very definition of "busy work," unable to replicate the classroom experience given the communal, collaborative aspects of modern education. These approaches also really minimized the role of the school librarian, many of whom were poised to help teachers work online by identifying potential applications and resources for distance learning. But perhaps most frustrated were the house-bound parents who found themselves forced into the *de facto* role of teacher; almost immediately, many took to social media to praise the real work of professional teachers, newly recognizing the skill implicit in effective instruction, especially for a whole class of learners with a range of abilities and needs. Many educators noted that what parents were undertaking was not homeschooling in the accepted sense of the word, but instead crisis learning, a stop-gap designed to maintain some sense of routine and connection with the classroom, especially for students who would not return that school year.

In one of my professional learning communities, the one question everyone seemed to be getting from students was about returning materials. Would the books be overdue? How would they pay the fines? We all laughed at the misunderstanding of librarians' concern that this represented, but I thought about this small anxiety in the shadow of larger ones, and wanted everyone to update their websites with reassurances. And I wanted to train school librarians who had automated overdues to turn off those emails remotely.

It is natural that parents want to maintain normalcy, especially for their children, in the face of uncertainty. When school is disrupted, be it for a national disaster, a disease outbreak, or severe weather, children still retain their need for structure and the sense of regularity imposed by daily routine. It might seem natural to transfer the same schedule into another context, but the limitations of attempting to cover the same variety and scope of standards-based content at home quickly becomes evident. Younger children, especially, find uncertainty challenging, and do not naturally adopt a "wait and see" attitude.

New Routines

Parents, while maintaining a daily routine, can use these moments as an opportunity to share their own skills and abilities with children. I noticed several schoolteacher friends emphasizing that they were not expecting their own children to do any approximation of class work, but were instead using the time for independent reading, to cook and bake together, to do arts and crafts, and to share family histories. These were all things that theoretically could be done anytime, but were too often overlooked in the day-to-day bustle or relegated to enrichment instead of core curriculum. Other parents embraced a constructive, if dated, use of media, exposing their children to videos fondly remembered from their own childhoods like *Schoolhouse Rock* and using *Little House on the Prairie* for history lessons. Families took socially distanced walks together to maintaining physical activity, or tapped into a range of indoor exercise and yoga videos and synchronous online classes. Though the pandemic provided teachable moments in everything from media literacy to historical theory of disease, for many, it seemed necessary to limit time spent on social media and limit consumption of news and potential disinformation.

There are other students and households that will be less directly affected and will see school closures (for anything from predicated inclement weather that fails to materialize, to outbreaks of flu or other illness) as "an abundance of caution." In environments where these decisions on the parts of local governments have been highly politicized, it is essential that teacher monitor the tenor of the conversation both remotely and upon return to school to prevent bullying and provide insight into the duty of care provided by schools. The school climate should remain safe for the students who may have been affected the most by any disruption.

In the midst of the 2020 outbreak, there was a lot of tension around the topic of public libraries in particular closing to protect their front-line staffers. Given the dire pronouncements about economic depression to follow, no doubt many library administrators wanted to position themselves as essential services for future budgets. But maintaining a sense of normalcy meant that many librarians found creative ways to connect online, and in-person programming morphed into streaming storytimes, collection analysis and diversity audits proceeded remotely, highly local curated resources were developed and promoted at a distance, and reference services were provided by social media and integrated chat functions.

TRAUMA SENSITIVITY

When students do return to school after prolonged closures, they will have been through ordeals we might not immediately appreciate. Students who are dependent on free or subsidized meals at school many have gone hungry, children may have experienced physical violence or emotional abuse as families were constrained in close quarters, and the immediate financial fallout of long-term closures may have affected their households. They may have lost family members or friends to the virus. Others will have deeply internalized the media messaging and will be reluctant to be in usual physical proximity to classmates. For many young people, this emotional distress will be a psychic scar they will carry long into adulthood. More immediately, many will be unable to resume school and will act out in response to the changes.

It is imperative that anytime school is disrupted, teachers acknowledge what students have been though and allocate and protect classroom time rebuilding the interpersonal connections that make school communities function. Similarly, when the school or class has lost a student, conversation about that can be the best use of instructional time. Diving right back into the curriculum may seem necessary after a protracted break, but often the outside events can function like "an elephant in the room," impossible to ignore and begging to be addressed, and it will be impossible to meet instructional objectives if the larger-scale events are not discussed.

School librarians were among those, during COVID-19 closures, tweeting about the #infodemic and noting the wide variation in information being disseminated, using analysis of soundbites and infographics as teachable moments, constructing hyper-local self-isolation memes, and plugging some of the more spurious theories into tools like Snopes to discredit their validity. Data literacy specialists seized on the variety of statistics and used the opportunity to discuss exponential growth and urban density. But much of the most inspiring librarian work was fueled with direct, albeit remote, connections to the school communities, including updates about local virus testing protocols and the provision of free services. The American Library Association's own statement urged libraries to keep the Wi-Fi accessible so that it could be used from outside the building if need be. School librarians who had not cultivated social media presences, either personally or for their library, did not have the immediate avenues of connections to students and teachers available for those who had worked to cultivate online presence.

While many school librarians are doing admirable work at a distance directing students and teachers to digitized resources, storytimes, and read-alouds, many generously posted by publishers without consideration of copyright, and using chat programs and online forms to connect with students off-campus, it is worthwhile to validate what children have been through in the long term. One way to do this is by planning to capture artifacts of the experience, like any event that becomes part of the school and class histories that should be reflected in its archives. Student journals can be preserved as primary sources; related newspapers and magazines can be saved for the inevitable future research projects.

Mindfulness, like any exercise, is best cultivated bit-by-bit and over time, but elements like body scanning and breath awareness can help even novices regain a sense of control in turbulent times. Mindfulness as a practice can support those in physical isolation, helping those to sit apart and quietly with themselves. More practically, it can make you more attuned to your physicality and help you avoid unhealthy behaviors like touching your face or potentially germ-ridden surfaces. But the basic mindfulness skills that can be cultivated in schools can support lifetimes of learning and living, improve focus and academic achievement, and promote health and wellbeing. In today's world, reflection and contemplation are perceived as a luxury for those crippled by self-absorption or a particular passion for self-improvement, but slowing down, being present, and focusing on ourselves and our work provides essential fodder for greater connection with both the human condition and local community, and at no time is this more evident than in moments of societal upheaval and uncertainty. We owe it to our school communities to provide this oasis of sanctuary.

Conclusion

As is the case with anything that is suddenly popular and increasingly ubiquitous, in this third decade of the twenty-first century, mindfulness, like wellness, can become something of a punchline, a knee-jerk reaction shifting responsibility onto individuals already overburdened by late-stage capitalization. Gwyneth Paltrow's GOOP newsletter, website, and subsequent television series are a prime example of the commodification of wellness trends. But human-centered mindfulness practice is an increasingly critical antidote to the technology-driven era in which we live.

The term Luddite, now used to deride those who reject technology, emerged from the movement of British weavers in the nineteenth century who faced obsolescence in the shadow of increasing mechanization. Ned Ludd was a weaver who famously rallied his colleagues in smashing stream-powered looms. But, over the past decade, the maker movement has confirmed how empowering it can be to master a skill and use it in constructive ways, even when mass-produced options are easier and less expensive. We owe it to our students to work on growing their stores of skill and knowledge; we are helping them learn the dispositions to learn, the most valuable skill in any future society and economy.

Last summer, I held a successful program at our university's Kids College that focused on the art of Louise Bourgeios and culminated in students making their own hand looms. While few people will ever weave fabrics for their own garments, practice in that process exposes you to a range of metaphors about production and the agency of creation. Today, when we consider the value of handmade objects over those created through mass production, it becomes clear that the slower, more artisanal ways have value and beauty not always present in larger-scale manufacturing. School libraries are ideally situated to slow down learning and help students experience the craft inherent in contemplation that can lead to invention.

Promoting mindfulness in institutional environments can seem to be an uphill battle. The technological revolution was late in coming to schools, but too often routinized, programmatic uses of technology edge out and ultimately replace human-centered teaching and learning. When I worked at a school that was well-known for improving student literacy, visitors would often want to know what programs or products our school had found to get those results. Our very patient assistant principal always stressed that each classroom teacher was using rather standard comprehension reading strategies that fit their objectives using a range of text the teachers had curated themselves, especially articles and trade books rather than the district-issued textbooks. There was also a terrific amount of intensive one-on-one instruction and small group intervention going on. This was never the quick fix other schools were looking for. Since then, more boards of education have chosen to invest in hardware and software that adapts to a student's performance. This is often described in terms of personalization, or more cynically, teacher-proofing the curriculum. Advocated of inquiry, project-based and active learning often urge the teacher to be "the guide on the side" rather than "the sage on the stage," but my worry is that the guide often becomes tech support with little real instructional role. If we abdicate our deeply human instructional role to machines, we will never get it back.

More and more parents are rejecting school experiences that are increasingly screen-based, reports Valerie Strauss in the *Washington Post*. Virtual schooling may be a solution for some students, but many more can benefit broadly by learning to nurture connections with each other. Our future as a society is predicated upon it. But in the same way that nineteenth century libraries were about literacy for the masses, twenty-first century libraries can be about literacy for the human condition and promote social emotional awareness and affinities between individuals.

One of the most chilling capabilities I have encountered related to augmented reality suggests that future interfaces would allow individuals to ignore the aspects of the community they did not want to see, enabling them to completely tune out poverty and homelessness, those with disabilities, and even those with differences. Rather than building empathy, these technologies have the potential to erase it.

School librarians can create inclusive spaces that promote care for ourselves, each other, our communities and the world around us as a daily practice as part of a necessary universe of support for young people. A colleague suggested that the recent trend for nature, like mindfulness, is driven by its relatively accessible price-point. If distributing some photo-copied coloring pages signals mindfulness, decorating with a few plants signals your library is embracing nature. But school libraries can be more mindful without any expenditure. I believe that the roots of mindfulness exist in reflection and planning on the part of open professionals who are themselves life-long learners assessing the climate and reconfiguring their praxis accordingly.

The school library is not for everyone. I had a student who taught PE at an elementary school; his first day observing in the library, he was dis-mayed at what he perceived as unchecked chaos in the space. While he was used to managing almost a hundred children at a time, the more free-form instruction and movement involved when classes came to the library threw him for a loop. While he completed his degree, he is still in his other position. Another friend recently returned to the English classroom after two years as a school librarian, citing the lack of any dedicated planning block as effectively resulting in her working 25 percent more for the same monetary compensation. That is a legitimate concern; vocational creep has left many librarians to try to be all things to all people. But her analy-sis was in terms of per-hour remuneration rather than embracing the expansive and whole-school role of a school librarian. And, because library cultures are so school-specific, it is possible to thrive in one envi-ronment and wither in another. I do think we have to consider our own dispositions and make sure that we are in the right spaces for our own types of work.

School library settings are unique in the lack of administrative layers involved in everything from ordering to programming that can make working in other library setting more frustrating. School librarians need to embrace that latitude and craft spaces, programs, and services that reflect student and teacher needs and promote critical human connections. When I ask my former students, even those who are practicing librarians, what they want their libraries to be, too often they have not considered any change as being within their purview. They accept the library "as is," and work around any impediments of the physical space or established prac-tice. When each county in my state introduced a Pre-K program, it was astonishing how few librarians made any provision for these youngest stu-dents in terms of collections, services, or schedule; given the emphasis on increasing school readiness, especially for those from disadvantaged backgrounds, it seemed critical that the Pre-K students have access to library resources.

One easy starting point in working toward mindfulness is taking care of yourself and modeling healthy work-life balance for your students and colleagues. If you are lucky enough to have colleagues or paraprofessionals in the library, one of the most effective things you can do is ensure each other take breaks and not work beyond set hours. Because they feel such heavy responsibility for their space and role, I know many librarians who will not leave until every book is shelved and every chair pushed in. We have to realize that this sort of housekeeping is not our real work.

When I first became a school librarian, it was a perpetual joke that whenever I tried to get something done in the workroom or storage areas, I would immediately be requested in the library proper. It was such a busy place that I never had time away from the desk. I excused not stopping for lunch as not liking to eat midday and saw not taking time off as a demonstration of commitment to the community or teachers and students who sought my expertise. With hindsight, after almost 15 years without a midday break, I realized how much less tired I might have been in the evenings if I had taken that half hour to read, to sit in the dark, as one of my colleagues managed to do, or had gone for an invigorating walk around campus, which would have also allowed me to observe instruction and consider possible interventions. Sometimes, it is necessary to remove yourself from the situation, in the same way it can be beneficial for students to take a break from the classroom to come to the library.

Whatever your approach to slowing down your instruction and creating connections across the curriculum, making your space more welcoming and inclusive, or adjusting your collections to better reflect your readers and your community, mindfulness is present in the concepts that underpin reflective educational practice. By supporting those in your building and recognizing and nurturing your own needs, you are bound to find your work more rewarding and less draining. I hope this book provides some fodder for your work and increases the satisfaction and decreases the stress of one of the most important jobs in the school, and helps you to create a space and atmosphere where all students have a respite from the stresses and the unrelenting pace of contemporary education.

Annotated Bibliography

BOOKS

Bizzle, Ben, and Maria Flora. *Start a Revolution: Stop Acting Like a Library.* **Chicago, IL: ALA Editions, 2015.**
Bizzle's punchy guide to marketing the great things going on in your library includes drilling down to patron-centered initiatives and communications and persuasive strategies for gaining administrative support for nonconventional initiatives.

Campana, Kathleen, J. Elizabeth Mills, and Susan Hildreth. *Create, Innovate, and Serve: A Radical Approach to Children's and Youth Programming.* **Chicago, IL: ALA Neal-Schuman, 2019.**
This volume collocates the work of a range of the most proactive professionals in librarianship for young people. Play and making are treated as serious subjects, and exemplary programs across the nation are detailed by those who created them.

Charney, Madeleine, Jenny Colvin, and Richard Moniz. *Recipes for Mindfulness in Your Library: Supporting Resilience and Community Engagement.* **Chicago, IL: ALA Editions, 2019.**
Zen zones, brain booths, yoga, meditation, and rest are all explored by contributors to this pithy volume replete with a range of personal practice and programming for a range of populations.

Domine, Vanessa Elaine. *Healthy Teens, Healthy Schools: How Media Literacy Education Can Renew Education in the United States.* **Lanham, MD: Rowman & Littlefield, 2015.**

Beginning with the long history of the press and public health and morality efforts, Domine presents communitarian and politically neutral ways to promote holistic well-being.

Gray, David. *Liminal Thinking: Create the Change You Want by Changing the Way You Think*. Brooklyn, NY: Two Waves Books, 2016.
Gray's book deals with challenging our ingrained belief system, living in the moment, and using storytelling to build empathy and connection.

Holland, Eva. *Nerve: Adventures in the Science of Fear*. New York: The Experiment, 2020.
This very personal exploration is supported by the physiology and mental process underpinning fear and gets at the difficulty and necessity of confronting triggers associated with past trauma.

Honore, Carl. *In Praise of Slowness: Challenging the Cult of Speed*. New York: HarperCollins, 2004.
Honore immerses himself in counterculture challenges to modernity in many areas of contemporary life. Of particular interest is Chapter Ten, looking at parenting "the unhurried child" through "slow schooling," including contrasting international approaches to education.

Johnson, Ranae. *Reclaim Your Light through the Miracle of Rapid Eye Technology*. Salem, OR: Ranae Johnson, 2002.
Like tapping, Johnson's rapid eye technology technique attempts to harness physical inputs to access emotional responses, in this case excavating underlying feelings to promote healing.

Kondo, Marie, and Scott Sonenshein. *Joy at Work: Organizing Your Professional Life*. New York: Little, Brown Spark, 2020.
This volume brings Kondo's revolutionary tidying process to the work world, including sorting and managing time and digital work, evaluating contacts, and gathering meetings, all with the intention of paring back to the essential and giving yourself some breathing room.

McGee, Kristin. *Chair Yoga: Sit, Stretch, and Strengthen Your Way to a Happier, Healthier You.* **New York: HarperCollins Publishers, 2017.**
McGee modifies many common yoga poses and breath work for seated practitioners. The photographs that illustrate the volume are easy to follow and share with whole class groups.

Moniz, Richard, Joe Eshleman, Jo Henry, Howard Slutzky, and Lisa Moniz. *The Mindful Librarian: Connecting the Practice of Mindfulness to Librarianship.* **Waltham, MA: Chandos Publishing, an imprint of Elsevier, 2016.**
With the academic library setting in mind, this work includes consideration of mindfulness as it applies to reference, instruction, relationships with faculty, and library leadership, ultimately presenting mindfulness as an antidote to burnout, especially among solo practitioners.

Neese, Ashley. *How to Breathe: 25 Simple Practices for Calm, Joy and Resilience.* **Berkeley, CA: Ten Speed Press, 2019.**
Neese approaches breathwork as an accessible practice using combinations of inhalation and exhalation to address a variety of physical and emotional concerns, closing with reflection and journaling to strengthen the mind-body connection.

Nhat Hanh, Thich. *Mindfulness Essentials Series.* **Berkeley, CA: Parallax Press, 2015.**
This beautifully illustration pocket-sized five book series—*How to Sit, How to Eat, How to Love, How to Walk,* and *How to Relax*—is full of page-long meditations that can act as bellringers in classroom settings.

Odell, Jenny. *How to Do Nothing: Resisting the Attention Economy.* **Brooklyn, NY: Melville House, 2019.**
Odell plumbs the complicated relationships between being human, living in nature, and a scarcity of time and attention in the modern landscape of unrelenting productivity.

Reale, Michelle. *Becoming a Reflective Librarian and Teacher: Strategies for Mindful Academic Practice.* **Chicago, IL: ALA Editions, 2017.**

Intentionality, authenticity, and autobiography are aspects of the reflective practice Reale highlights, using iterative approaches like journaling and concept-mapping for ongoing self-assessment.

Smallwood, Carol. *Bringing the Arts into the Library*. Chicago, IL: ALA Editions, 2014.
This collection of essays showcases successful incorporation of literary, visual, and performing arts in a variety of library settings, including the behind-the-scenes management and administration supporting these sorts of efforts.

Smallwood, Carol, Julia L. Eisenstein, and Linda Burkey Wade. *Job Stress and the Librarian: Coping Strategies from the Professionals*. Jefferson, NC: McFarland & Company, 2013.
This collection of essays deals with perennially occurring issues ranging from managing conflict and burnout to promoting activity and nutrition to counteract stress. The toll of austerity and lack of administrative support are also addressed.

Stephens, Michael T. *The Heart of Librarianship: Attentive, Positive, and Purposeful Change*. Chicago, IL: ALA Editions, 2016.
Stephens explores the empathetic side of the profession, including the soft skills necessary for librarian success and deep career satisfaction. He stresses getting beyond the "citation fixation" to create a culture of life-long learning.

Stephens, Michael T. *Wholehearted Librarianship: Finding Hope, Inspiration, and Balance*. Chicago, IL: ALA Editions, 2019.
Stephens discusses the role of compassion as a facet of library work, creating a participatory service culture, and the potential role of *hygge* in generating sanctuary and community within library spaces.

Stoltz, Dorothy. *Inspired Collaboration: Ideas for Discovering and Applying Your Potential*. Chicago, IL: ALA Editions, 2016.
Rather than focusing on instructional collaboration with classroom teachers, Stoltz offers a variety of ways that community groups and initiatives can support each other and thrive together, with a focus on sustainable community engagement and long-term partnerships.

Stoltz, Dorothy, Morgan Miller, Lisa Picker, Joseph Thompson, and Carrie Willson. *Inspired Thinking: Big Ideas to Enrich Yourself and Your Community.* Chicago, IL: ALA Editions, 2020.
In this philosophic treatise, Stoltz et al. situate librarianship inside a larger history of ideas and link daily work to creativity and community.

Sykes, Judith A. *Brain Friendly School Libraries.* Westport, CT: Libraries Unlimited, 2006.
The many roles of a school librarian, from staff developer to cultural emissary, are explored with a range of practical and easy-to-implement suggestions to support brain development in young people through spaces, collections, and library planning.

Turkle, Sherry. *Reclaiming Conversation: The Power of Talk in a Digital Age.* New York: Penguin Books, 2016.
Turkle questions the received wisdom of deferring to the algorithms that define modern life, positing that it is by putting machines aside and focusing on interpersonal interaction that we will work toward both healthier relationships and increased insight and self-reflection.

ARTICLES

Cellucci, Anita. "How My School Library Embraces Social Emotional Learning." *School Library Journal.* February 2, 2017. https://www.slj.com/?detailStory=how-my-school-library-embraces-social-emotional-learning.
Cellucci, who styles herself "the Empathetic Librarian," outlines mental health support, bibliotherapeutic approaches, and routes to student empowerment in her high school library.

Clay, Erica. "Social Emotional Learning Happens in Your Library." *Teach With INFOhio.* April 7, 2017. https://www.infohio.org/blog/item/social-emotional-learning-happens-in-your-library.
Clay collocates a range of resources related to SEL and stresses the importance of collaboration and advocacy in these efforts.

Cooksey, Ashley. "Mindful Space in the Library." *Knowledge Quest* **(blog). September 14, 2018.** https://knowledgequest.aasl.org/mindful-space-in-the-library/.
Cooksey proposes app-supported yoga and meditation for teachers as well as students.

Jacobson, Linda. "Teach Students Resilience, Empathy, and More with Social Emotional Learning Strategies." *School Library Journal.* **February 2, 2017.** https://www.slj.com/?detailStory=teach-students-resilience-empathy-and-more-with-social-emotional-learning-strategies.
Jacobson investigates whole-school programmatic efforts for SEL, including research that supports its efficacy in approving student achievement.

Phillips, Abigail Leigh. "Understanding Empathetic Services: The Role of Empathy in Everyday Library Work." *The Journal of Research on Libraries and Young Adults* **8, no.1 (July 2017).** http://www.yalsa.ala.org/jrlya/2017/07/understanding-empathetic-services-the-role-of-empathy-in-everyday-library-work/.
Grounded in Phillips' dissertation research (*The Empathetic Librarian: Rural Librarians as a Source of Support for Rural Cyberbullied Young Adults*, ProQuest Number: 10120555), this paper investigates the types of emotional support that rural school and public librarians provide young people.

Robinson, Alice A. "Mastering Mindfulness: Fostering a Mindfulness Culture in Children." *Children and Libraries* **18, no. 1 (Spring 2020): 17–18.**
Robinson outlines a series of read-alouds to promote character education she has used to promote interpersonal connection and kindness in her junior high school library.

ONLINE RESOURCES

The Collaborative for Academic, Social, and Emotional Learning (CASEL). https://casel.org/
In its mission to disseminate high-quality SEL strategies and approaches, CASEL aims to support districts, schools, and state-wide initiatives to drive research, guide practice, and inform policy.

Let's Move Libraries. http://letsmovelibraries.org/.

> Curated by LIS professor Noah Lenstra, Let's Move Libraries offers program ideas infused with physical activity for all sorts of demographics including StoryWalks, yoga classes, gardens, and the circulation of fitness equipment.

MindUP. https://mindup.org/.

> This project of Goldie Hawn's foundation seeks to teach children the skills they need "to regulate their stress and emotion, form positive relationships, and act with kindness and compassion, focusing on four areas: Neuroscience, Positive Psychology, Mindful Awareness, and Social-Emotional Learning. In addition to resources, the site includes research studies analyzing the efficacy of this approach.

The Morningside Center for Teaching Social Responsibility. https://www.morningsidecenter.org/.

> Offers a wide range of lessons and resources, the majority of which deal with teachable moments in social responsibility and restorative practices.

RULER. http://ei.yale.edu/ruler/ruler-overview/.

> Yale University's Center for Emotional Intelligence says RULER seeks to apply "hard science" to the teaching of what have historically been called "soft skills." Designed for whole-school implementation, it includes the MoodMeter that helps students pinpoint and name emotions, the first an initial step toward mindfulness.

Stories, Songs, and Stretches. https://www.storiessongsandstretches.com/.

> Katie Scherrer, who had provided professional development for librarians via InfoPeople webinars, provides resources, including YouTube videos, about storytimes for children and adults and her workshops for those interested in facilitating yoga storytimes in libraries.

Stressed Teens. https://www.stressedteens.com/.

> A project of therapist Gina M. Biegel, Stressed Teens offers online professional development and workshops promoting mindfulness-based stress reduction for teens, including a number of free resources.

Trauma Sensitive Schools. https://traumasensitiveschools.org/.

The Trauma and Learning Policy Initiative's mission is "to ensure that children traumatized by exposure to family violence and other adverse childhood experiences succeed in school," which it approaches through the lens of policy and whole-school cultural change. Includes two downloadable book-length resources in its series, *Helping Traumatized Children Learn.*

Wellness in the Library Resources. https://nnlm.gov/gmr/guides /wellness-library-workplace-resources

This collections of resources and toolkits is curated by librarian Bobbi Newman, Community Engagement and Outreach Specialist for National Network of Libraries of Medicine's Greater Midwest Region, showcasing Medline and NIH resources related to many aspects of workplace health.

Yoga in My School. https://yogainmyschool.com/.

Donna Freeman designed Yoga in My School primarily as a password-protected member community and professional development platform for teachers using age-appropriate pedagogy, with many applicable to library settings, including Yoga for Literacy. There are a few freely accessible resources, including tips on teaching yoga to large groups and podcasts.

Yoga in the Library. https://www.yogainthelibrary.com/.

This website—developed by Jenn Carson, director of the L.P. Fisher Public Library in Woodstock, New Brunswick, blogged extensively about Yoga in the Library for ALA—includes embedded videos of library-based programs and practice and printable resources.

APPS

There are an abundance of apps which offer guided meditations for beginners, and the majority are subscription-based apps with free trials. **Calm** has a high profile and is currently running television advertisements. It has offered free accounts for teachers in the past, but its classroom option is currently not taking new applicants.

An Australian project with a significant foundation in research, **Smiling Mind** includes a meditation app developed specifically for young people, and it is free.

Former Buddhist monk Andy Puddicombe, whose TED Talk on Meditation, "All It Takes Is Ten Minutes," https://www.ted.com/talks/andy _puddicombe_all_it_takes_is_10_mindful_minutes, is an excellent introduction to the practice, and has attained something of a cult following narrating the **Headspace** sessions. It is easy to sign up for **Headspace's** free educator option.

Ten Percent offers both audio and video meditation options in its free tier of services and allows you to choose an experience based on how long you plan to spend meditating.

Unlike most subscription-based meditation apps, **Stop, Think and Breathe** does not require a credit card for trial access and offers a range of free meditations, directing to you to a session based on an initial survey.

Insight Timer offers 3,000 guided meditation sessions categorized by emotional need and includes a dedicated track for kids.

UCLA's **Mindful** is an app offering free guided meditations in both English and Spanish.

Though not a mediation app per se, the **Pause** app uses a calming soundtrack (which can be layered over other audio) as a backdrop for sessions from one to thirty minutes, using your fingers as a cursor to race the meditative path of an on-screen dot, forcing you to maintain contact and gently urging you to slow down or speed up the process as required. It is like Tai Chi for your fingertips.

The **Mood Meter** app, developed by RULER, Yale's Center for Emotional Intelligence, allows users to check in along two axes mapped toward energy and positivity. The app allows for tracking and contrast over time, but this can also work offline with printed charts, establishing a shared vocabulary for emotion and feeling.

ASMRtist is an app that allows you to combine a wide variety of soothing ambient noises and set a timer for a very personal relaxation soundtrack.

Index

About the Author

Wendy Stephens, PhD, is assistant professor and school library chair at Jacksonville State University. Before joining the faculty at Jacksonville, Stephens was a high school librarian for 15 years.

CPSIA information can be obtained
at www.ICGtesting.com
Printed in the USA
JSHW050252240622
27306JS00003B/12